Castles, Mystery and Music

Castles, Mystery and Music

The Legend of Ludwig II

A Pictorial History of the Life
of Ludwig II of Bavaria
by Anton Sailer

Bruckmann München

Jacket/Front:
King Ludwig II at a Knighting Ceremony.
Gouache, attributed to Friedrich Eibner, c. 1875.

Jacket/Back:
Design for Falkenstein Castle.
Gouache by Christian Jank, 1883.

Opposite the title:
King Ludwig II in the uniform of a Bavarian General.

Translation from the German by Sheila Ickerott

Original title: Bayerns Märchenkönig
Published by F. Bruckmann KG, München
ISBN 3 7654 1894 3

CIP-Kurztitelaufnahme der Deutschen Bibliothek:
Bayerns Märchenkönig: d. Leben Ludwigs II. in Bildern/
Anton Sailer. – 3., völlig überarb. Aufg. –
München: Bruckmann, 1983.
ISBN 3-7654-1894-3
NE: Sailer, Anton (Hrsg).

© 1961/1983 Verlag F. Bruckmann KG, München
All rights reserved
Published by F. Bruckmann KG, München
Graphische Kunstanstalten
Printed in Germany
ISBN 3 7654 1898 6

Contents

Ludwig, the First Son born to the Bavarian Crown Prince Maximilian

To the Bavarian Crown Prince Maximilian and his wife Marie was born on 25th August 1845 at 28 minutes past midnight at Nymphenburg, the summer residence of the royal family, their first son. Gods and demigods witnessed from the ceiling of the great hall at Nymphenburg the ceremonial baptismal of the Wittelsbach heir on the following day. The rumour circulated in Munich, however, that the birth had been kept a secret for two days in order to please the baby's grandfather, Ludwig I, whose birthday and name day was on 25th August.

Whether there was any truth in this or not, it is significant that the myth around Ludwig originated from the very day of his birth. An entranced dream world and cold reality, dazzling splendour and sombre tragedy form a fateful mixture in the life of the Dream King, who loved his country of Bavaria – and to whose memory this book, an endeavour to document by means of pictures the Unforgotten, is dedicated.

8

The Royal Family

Ludwig I abdicated voluntarily on 20th March 1848 after his romance with Lola Montez; the three-year-old Ludwig became Crown Prince. A few weeks after Maximilian's accession to the throne, on 27th April, his second son, Otto, was born. In contrast to Ludwig, who even as a child showed his desire to command and whose nature bore the stamp of genius, Otto had a bright disposition, taking after his mother, and this made him her favourite. Erich Correns portrayed the royal family in the garden of the castle at Hohenschwangau *(opposite page)*. Both these charming, graceful children had a place in the hearts of the Bavarian people.

A Wittelsbach Characteristic

"He's keen on building like me!"enthused Ludwig I when his grandson Ludwig built and rebuilt towers with a set of building bricks after receiving them as a Christmas present in 1850. And when the court painter, Ernst Wilhelm Rietschel, portrayed the daydreaming Crown Prince, this game had to be included in the delicate water-colour.

Ludwig's Childhood

The Queen loved to feed the swans with her children *(opposite page)*. Their majesty made such an impression on Ludwig that he liked to draw swans *(right)*. His awareness of rank and his own prerogative was fostered by the excessive servility of his attendants: the sentence, "Meilhaus and Herr Klaß prostrate themselves at your feet" appeared in a letter from the eight-year-old Ludwig to his mother *(below)*. He also demanded this servility, and regarded even his brother Otto as his "vassal". It was in Berchtesgaden that he gagged Otto with the intention of "executing" him on the grounds of "insubordination". The heavy punishment he received for this instilled him with a dislike for Berchtesgaden which never left him.

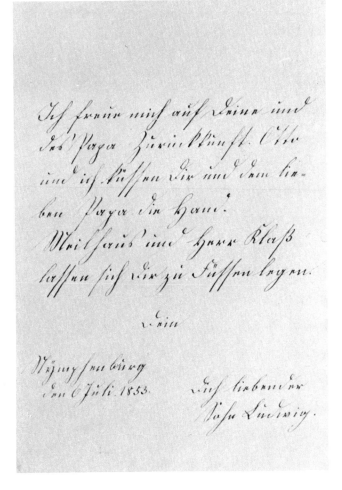

Ludwig's Youth

King Maximilian *(left)* was a modest, extremely conscientious ruler who patronized science and literature. He tended towards puritanical strictness at home; the timetable for Ludwig's private schooling had to be rigidly adhered to, and his erratic performance was punished with excessive severity. All intercourse with other children was denied Ludwig; his personality was to develop "in stillness". The syllabus aimed at a general education, but it was so extensive and so ponderous that no sound learning was to be gained. Another serious problem was the incredibly frugal diet then common in refined circles. The Crown Prince never had enough to eat, and it was to these inadequate meals that he was later able to attribute his rapid tooth decay. It was of little use that the good Liesl, an elderly chambermaid, slipped him the remains of her meals and even secretly bought him food. He also grew up to be completely unworldly: he never had to handle money, and when he came of age and was given his first purse containing about 50 marks, he wanted to buy up the contents of a jeweller's shop for his mother – not understanding why this was impossible. No wonder he later did not like to recall his restricted youth. Ludwig, tall, pale and lean, was left much of the time to himself, and he sought refuge in visionary dreams. His mother did not understand him. She was an uncomplicated woman, doubtless kindhearted, but without any intellectual aspirations. The Princes' confessor was the Abbot Haneberg, a good, intelligent, open-minded man who converted the Queen to Catholicism in 1874.

The Queen, a lovely Princess of Prussia, felt very much at home in the naturalness of the Alpine scenery. At that time it was not yet normal for ladies to ramble in the mountains; she did so and invented a stylish outfit for the purpose – under which the practical trousers showed. She also liked to see her children in walking clothes *(opposite page)*, when she could take them up to an alm, or even higher into a world of rocky peaks to gather edelweiss. This was – how could it be otherwise – the favourite flower of Marie, the first lady hiker from Berlin in the Bavarian Alps.

Decisive Impressions: Swans and Romance

In the Swan-knights' Hall at Hohenschwangau, Ludwig became familiar with the Lohengrin saga. He could stand for hours in front of 'Lohengrin's Farewell' *(below)* particularly, in which the castle at Hohenschwangau and the Alpsee form the background. In the Tasso Room, his father's bedroom, he could follow the story of Rinaldo and Armida *(left)*, and when he looked down onto the castle garden, he could see a glittering fountain of water shooting out of the beak of a swan set among rose bushes. This and the dream-world romance of the castle nurtured Ludwig's fantasy.

After years of pleading King Max at last permitted his son to see the opera 'Lohengrin'. It was 1861; Ludwig was sixteen and he abandoned himself to an unbridled, feverish passion. He had already read Wagner secretly, now he literally learned all his works by heart and devoured his prose, of which 'The Art Work of the Future' made the greatest impression on him. He had happened to see this work lying on Herzog Max's piano and it was lent to him with a smile – for who could take Wagner seriously? His art master was asked

to design costumes and scenery from the Wagnerian world according to his specifications, and when out walking he kept a lookout for "Lohengrin types". All this could not escape notice, but everyone regarded his passion for Wagner as a harmless caprice which would pass. Ludwig, however, was completely enchanted, and whenever he had to go out through the castle gates at Hohenschwangau into the real world, he applied his wonderful powers of fantasy to creating a parallel world – his own dream world.

Wilful and high-spirited – Crown Prince Ludwig in 1862.

The lions fountain in the castle gardens; cast in iron, a work by Ludwig Schwanthaler

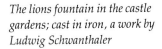

View from the romantic castle gates of Hohenschwangau

Death of Maximilian II
and Ludwig's Accession to the Throne

Maximilian II on his death-bed. The Queen, Crown Prince Ludwig and Prince Otto are saying their farewells.
Opposite page: Ludwig II in coronation robes.

Maximilian II, who had been ailing for some years, was convalescing in Italy at the end of 1863 when the political situation forced him to return home. The death of King Frederick VII of Denmark led to Prussia and Austria going to war over Schleswig-Holstein. Within the German Confederation, which was based on the equality of the partners, Prussia and Austria were vying for predominance – in the meantime they joined forces against Denmark. It was in this dispute that the modernized Prussian army proved itself – and from then on the South stood in awe of Prussian drill and organization. Bavaria, however, opposed this war and its consequences from the beginning. The tense situation literally consumed Maximilian's remaining strength, and, after a short illness, he finally took to his bed on 9th March 1864. On the next day the doctors gave up all hope, and Maximilian received the last rites calmly. After this he spoke with the Crown Prince. They were alone.

Prior to this, however, when he received the viaticum at five o'clock in the morning, the Frauenkirche's Benno bell summoned Munich to pray for its monarch – an irresistible call to a stunned people. In increasing numbers they crowded into the *Residenz*, the town palace, filling the courtyards, staircases and antechambers, and so Maximilian died amongst his large 'family'. He breathed his last at fifteen minutes before noon, holding the Queen's hands between his own and with his sons kneeling before him. Archbishop Gregorius von Scherr entered the antechamber and proclaimed in a clear voice: 'He is in heaven! We have lost a good king, let us pray that his son will prove his equal!' When Ludwig finally emerged from the death chamber, a courtier bowed to him with the words: 'Your Majesty!' This cut him like a whiplash; he blanched. His rule had begun. The last wish of his father, that he should enjoy an equally peaceful death, came to nothing, however...

'God will not desert Bavaria'

proclaimed the provost Ignaz von Döllinger *(left)* when Maximilian was buried on 14th March. He concluded his memorial address with an appeal to the people's loyalty, warning them not to 'drive the thorns of mistrust and fear' into the head of the young monarch as 'we need a monarchy as steadfast as an oak in a storm'. Was he, as some maintained, putting a check on plans for a deposition? But the Bavarian people were not lacking in real affection for their young monarch; they fell in love with him as he followed his father's coffin – pale, with dark, melting eyes. Ludwig II took the traditional oath in the council of state, which was presided over by his uncle Prince Luitpold. His earnestness, his dignity, affected the council; and while tears gathered in the eyes of the councillors Ludwig, 'handsome and majestic in the radiance of youth' addressed the following words to the Minister of State von Schrenck: "Almighty God has taken my much-loved father from this earth. I cannot express the feelings in my breast. The task that is now mine is great and difficult; I hope to God that He will grant me the grace and strength to fulfil it. I wish to reign true to the oath I now

take and in the spirit of the constitution, proven over nearly half a century. The welfare of my beloved people and the greatness of Bavaria will constitute my main endeavours. I count on your support in the fulfilment of my weighty duties."

Ludwig's shy politeness, his touching question when faced with a problem, "What would my father have done?" had led some of the gentlemen from the ministry – appointed by Maximilian – to underestimate the new King. They not only lacked due respect but imagined they could ignore Ludwig's commands and force their own opinions on him. They quickly came to an agreement with each other and were firmly convinced that Ludwig did not possess the courage nor the energy to assert himself. A decision of the King's, made completely independently a few weeks later, came like a bolt from the blue: he coolly ordered his first changes in the Cabinet. He spoke out against 'bureaucratic mutiny', threw two gentlemen out immediately, and forced the Freiherr von Schrenck *(right)* to resign. Maximilian had also thought him incompetent and he had been the one to advance furthest against Ludwig. The 34-year-old head of the Cabinet, Franz Xaver Pfistermeister, remained to become an influential figure: he was a conservative *Altbayer* from the Upper Palatinate, the son of a village teacher, dutiful and reliable.

A Nineteen-year-old Youth, all Heart and Soul

Important contemporaries agree that Ludwig was the most engaging of monarchs, and they all emphasize that the King's heart was 'pure and untainted'. Liberal observers such as the representative Graf Hegnenberg-Dux, however, watched uneasily as he enjoyed more and more "the delights of divine monarchy". Since 1848, monarchial power had been further limited by a State Basic Law – but there were government officials who encouraged Ludwig's youthful enthusiasm, his strong desire for complete sovereignty, and one of these was the Ministerial Assessor, Johann Lutz. Only later did it become evident that he was driven solely by his personal ambition, when he turned against his King with disastrous results. Another figure deserves a mention here: Graf Max Holnstein. He was an adventurer who made unscrupulous use of the chances given him. Holnstein – who was the result of an affair between Kurfürst Karl Albrecht and a lady-in-waiting – married into money and was able to persuade Ludwig to make him his chief equerry. Although, or perhaps because his character contrasted completely with that of the King, he maintained his influence and was to play a rôle as the "chief stableboy" – as he was known to the people of Munich. For the time being Ludwig zealously attended to his duties. Pfistermeister had to report to him regularly at 9 o'clock, and he often sent several times a day to the Cabinet to ask if there was anything new for him to sign. He liked to go on long, hard rides, and – which was overemphasized by his critics – he was fond of violets. That he was

The Men around the Young King

Johann Lutz, an ambitious man who made a career for himself under Ludwig and later thought himself indispensable.

Graf von Hegnenberg-Dux, a straightforward, dauntless character. He became Minister-President in 1871 but died in 1872.

Cabinet Secretary von Pfistermeister, the upright civil servant type. At 34 he initiated the King into his duties.

not a drinker, however, was an observation made by Bismarck *(right)* when he met Ludwig as Crown Prince. In August 1863 he was placed beside Ludwig at a banquet in Nymphenburg. He noted the following: "...During pauses in the conversation he stared past his mother at the ceiling and occasionally hastily emptied his glass of champagne. The refilling of his glass was slow, presumably on his mother's orders, and Ludwig frequently had to hold his empty glass over his shoulder where it was hesitantly filled; neither then or later did he overstep the bounds of moderation. I did, however, have the feeling that his surroundings bored him and that he encouraged his fantasy to escape from them with the aid of champagne..."

Much was to become deadly boring to Ludwig, but he was not yet to avoid the public eye. He was to be seen at the Corpus Christi procession *(below)* and at the *Oktoberfest*, at the theatre and in the streets in his carriage or on foot. Everything would have been perfect if he had not, shortly after his accession, called a "demon" to Munich: Richard Wagner.

Richard Wagner

The swan and cross became Ludwig's seal after his first 'Lohengrin' experience, and shortly after his accession he sent Pfistermeister off to look for Richard Wagner. He should present him with a portrait of the King and a ring with a ruby – for just as this ruby glowed so was Ludwig aglow with a desire to meet the creator of 'Lohengrin'. Pfistermeister went to Vienna only to find Wagner's house seized by his creditors. Nothing remained apart from 100 bottles of champagne, and those only because the creditors could not believe that these belonged to someone so much in debt. The Secretary was permitted to take a pencil and pen that the composer had used; finally, after a search that took him through Switzerland, he tracked him down in Stuttgart. Suspecting a foolish joke when the 'Secretary to the King of Bavaria' was announced, Wagner would not see him. Pfistermeister was able to fulfil his task on the following day, however, and they both left for Munich immediately. Wagner, whose affairs could hardly have been worse, did not hesitate to take a first class ticket – a story always recounted later by the honest Pfistermeister as being "typical of his extravagance". On 4th May in the afternoon, Ludwig was able to gaze into Wagner's lined face. He was disappointed in the composer's appearance, he was also not prepared for the Saxonian accent. Nevertheless he inwardly pledged himself to be true to Wagner's work. As early as November 1864, this patron had decided to build a monumental theatre for the works of the man he so admired.

Above: Richard Wagner's letter of thanks to King Ludwig, dated 3rd May 1864.

Left: The composer. Wagner had led an agitated life full of hazards. After endless struggles he became the 'Hofkapellmeister' in Dresden, participated in the uprising of 1849, however, and fled to Zurich. For years there was a warrant out against him (see below; this appeared on 11th June 1853). But the revolutionary in him was long disappointed politically. The performance of his newly revised 'Tannhäuser' in Paris in 1861 provoked a theatre scandal; Wagner went to Vienna, only to flee after a few years from an army of stubborn creditors.

Wagner alerted the architect of the Zurich Polytechnic, Gottfried Semper, who came to Munich towards the end of the year and was received in audience by the King. Three years later he presented him with a model of the theatre (above) which gained Ludwig's enthusiastic approval. The site was to be on the *Isarhöhen*, like the Maximilianeum, with an approach from the north-east side of the *Residenz* via a new bridge. This boulevard was to be built later more to the north – the *Prinzregentenstraße* – but the *Festspielhaus* was to remain a chimera. The Cabinet was up in arms when it became known that the overall costs would be six million gulden, that and the stubborn resistance in Munich finally forced Ludwig to give up the idea. His royal powers were insufficient, and from this first great disappointment dated his dislike of his capital.

Naturally from the very first day Wagner was to meet with adversaries, both openly and secretly, but who was to care: the King paid his debts and was most generous to him. The first payment from the Treasury amounted to 18000 gulden, the next to 40000, and further loans followed, apart from a stipend of 4000 gulden. But trouble-making rumour told that these sums were much higher, and whether this was believed or not, one thing was sure: Ludwig was under a spell. A daring silhouette (right) captured this idea.

Wagner was also dazed by the change in his life, and with anxiety he wrote about the King: "...He is sadly so beautiful and so spiritual, so brilliant and full of feeling that I am afraid his life must dwindle away like a transient godlike dream in this base world... My happiness is quite shattering; if he only may live! It is an incredible miracle!"

Kunst und Gunst.

A Strange Friendship

The happiest period then began for Ludwig. He moved to his summer residence, Schloss Berg at Lake Starnberg (*below*), and Richard Wagner was housed a quarter of an hour's ride away.

A union of souls of the most ideal kind gave both memorable weeks, and Ludwig abandoned himself with eagerness to Richard Wagner's inexhaustible flow of words. The Master of tone and word used this time to persuade Ludwig to call Hans von Bülow, Peter Cornelius and other friends to Munich to give him support. In a colourful, glittering, fantastic costume, Wagner sat at a desk in the commodious Villa Pellet (*right*) and drew up a programme spanning many years that overpowered Ludwig. 'Tristan', 'The Mastersingers', the complete 'Ring', 'Parsifal' – of these the astonished youth could not hear enough. And yet Ludwig did not forget the affairs of state. The King received his ministers in Schloss Berg, fulfilling all the duties of his public life.

Elisabeth, Empress of Austria

First Meeting with Elisabeth

For four days only had Ludwig intended visiting the Emperor and Empress of Austria in Bad Kissingen in the middle of June – but he stayed four weeks without writing a single line to Richard Wagner. Remaining inwardly completely free, he devoted himself to the other prominent guests, to whom the Tsar and his consort belonged. The fashionable spa raved about him, and there was not one female who did not envy the Empress and the Tsarina that they could have this Apollo between them *(below)*. From this time onwards there was a deep and lasting bond between Ludwig and the beautiful Elisabeth. She was his elder by eight years, and with the instinct of a mature woman she presaged his fate, and bore his ardent admiration. He called her 'the Dove', while for her he was 'the Eagle' – but she wrote sorrowfully in her diary "poor King Ludwig". Yet although his attentions were always above reproach, he was playing with fire. It is only in the light of this meeting that Ludwig's later behaviour to Sophie, Elisabeth's younger sister, is to be seen. The days passed delightfully, Bad Kissingen spoiled its illustrious guest – and at Lake Starnberg sat Richard Wagner, lonely and offended. But Cosima, Bülow's wife is on her way with her children. When she arrives, a passionate woman is alone with the genius...

Below: Scene in front of Spa at Bad Kissingen.

Gossip and Scandal

After returning from Bad Kissingen, Ludwig soon left again to devote his attention to the Tsarina and her ten-year-old daughter in Bad Schwalbach. This physical separation from Wagner did not in any way cool his ardour, however. At the beginning of October Wagner moved into the house in the Briennerstrasse in Munich that the King had rented for him *(opposite page, above)*. It was then that the first rumours and grumbling started in Munich: Wagner's extravagant way of life was the first reason, but his familiar relationship with the elegant Cosima in her rustling silks prompted even more animosity. This ambitious, incredibly self-confident and intelligent woman captivated even personal enemies – but this was not the case with the King: he was extremely suspicious of her. Her husband's position was the worst, but Bülow was able to bear with composure the increasingly evident victory of the stronger. An extremely unwelcome figure for Wagner was the Music Director Franz Lachner *(right)*. This musician of the old school was to rehearse 'The Flying Dutchman' – whereupon he promptly became ill. Wagner eagerly took up the baton himself and carried his work to success. But despite this everyone was against him, the Court, the clergy, the government and the people – and yet, at Ludwig's command, 'Tristan' was put into rehearsal. Overcome, "borne by the most divine love", Richard Wagner wrote: "This happiness is the only thing that can wholly compensate for the wretched misery I have suffered".

*Wagner's house in Munich,
water-colour by L. Wolf Trautmann.*

Opposite page:

*Above left: Caricature from the Munich 'Punsch' illustrating
Richard Wagner's eternal need of money from the Cabinet.*

Above right: Richard Wagner and Cosima.

Below: Music Director Franz Lachner.

Right: Hans von Bülow.

*Caricature illustrating Bülow's scornful remark about the
"Schweinehunde".*

Ein paar Bülow'sche Sperrsitzreihen.

The Impudent Herr von Bülow

Even the most minute details were determined by Richard Wagner in preparation for the performance of the work that was considered unproduceable. Hans von Bülow was to undertake the musical direction of 'Tristan and Isolde'. Twenty-one orchestra rehearsals proved necessary, and the decorations and costumes swallowed astonishing sums. These circumstances became known and the press was poisoned even more against the 'Wagner clique', with Bülow also getting his share. When he wanted to enlarge the orchestra and was told that thirty seats would have to be sacrificed, he lost control and scornfully replied: "So what? Does it matter whether there are thirty *Schweinehunde* more or less in the theatre?" This *faux pas* brought Munich to boiling point. He did afterwards explain that it was not meant like that, and that in Berlin the expression *Schweinehund* was not offensive; but this explanation was not accepted and the *Bayerisches Volksblatt* summed up the general mood: "If Hans von Bülow, the prototype of real Prussian self-conceit and uncouthness, should happen to wander into the patriotic

rooms of the *Hofbräuhaus*, he would be lucky to get away with being quartered..."

This tense situation continued, and still the work progressed "like an enchanted dream ... to undreamt-of reality". Resistance was useless, and even though Munich had previously only known painters and poets to enjoy royal favour – Ludwig removed all seemingly insurmountable obstacles from Wagner's path and 'Tristan' arose. On 11th May 1865, Ludwig attended the final full rehearsal. On the same day he ordered his Minister of Justice to proclaim an amnesty for all those non-Bavarians involved in the 1849 revolution. This was a symbolic gesture with reference to Wagner, who had found asylum in Bavaria.

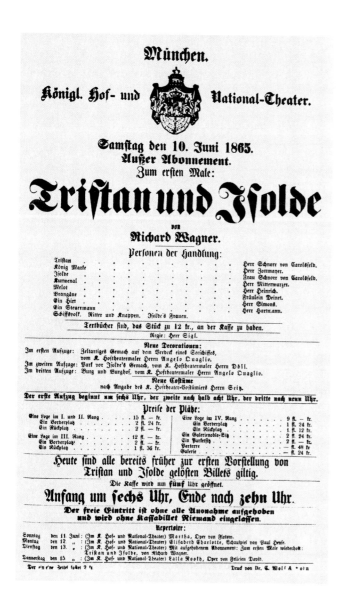

Triumph of the "Adventurer Musician"

The memorable programme for the great event that attracted so many to Munich.

Opposite page:
Tristan and Isolde, played by Ludwig and Malvine Schnorr von Carolsfeld.
Even during the rehearsals Wagner was beside himself with enthusiasm; he embraced the couple and did a headstand on a stage sofa for joy.

Bülow conducting, a caricature referring to him and Wagner's music.

Another ordeal was to come: Frau Schnorr von Carolsfeld, who played Isolde, fell ill, and the first performance had to be postponed. The wildest rumours were circulating, and it was said that Wagner had been arrested because of his debts on bills. It was true that his enemies wanted to bring about his fall in this way, but Ludwig did not hesitate to come to his rescue and pacified him in a warm letter; on 10th June the curtain at last rose on 'Tristan and Isolde' at the *Hoftheater* (Court Theatre). The King was greeted by a fanfare and cheers. The whole Court was there, although the stalls and the gallery only filled during the overture (a precaution taken to prevent a demonstration against Bülow). The applause came gradually. The Wagner fans naturally clapped after the first act, others hissed. It was only at the end that the hissing was drowned by enthusiastic applause: a triumph for Wagner, but also for Ludwig.

The Magic of Entrancement

The romantic 'Tristan' – which even Wagner thought a miracle and openly admitted: "How I could create something like this becomes increasingly inexplicable" – this Tristan was performed four times only. After the last performance, Ludwig pulled the emergency brake of his special train on his way back to Berg, and after he had taken the night air, continued his journey in the locomotive – a picture-book king. And no other monarch would have himself written a letter to an artist starting, "My only one! My godlike friend!" But Ludwig's letters to Wagner are also proof of a rapture which could only thrill the soul of an inwardly lonely person. Wagner read simply wholehearted admiration and a readiness to make sacrifices for the furthering of his work into these letters.

Above: Ludwig's expression was still unclouded when his thoughts dwelt on Richard Wagner; and he still wrote when his unquenchable desire for his own dream world overflowed.

Right: An estatic letter from the King to Wagner.

Opposite page: Wagner presented his magnanimous benefactor with this photograph; the dedication: "Only you give me the strength by your royal, steadfast belief in me, to thank you!"

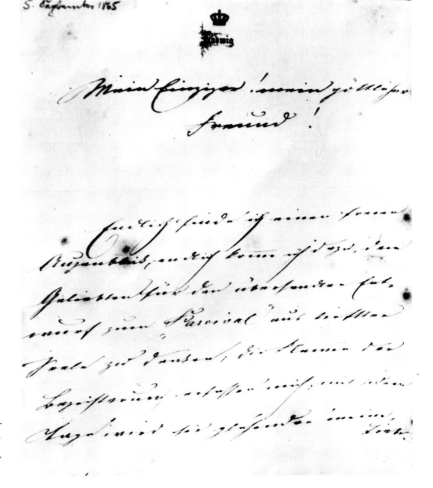

The Swan-knight on the Alpsee

The King's position forced him at the end to 1865 to put a check on his relationship with Wagner. Shortly before this, the friendship reached its zenith: at the beginning of November Wagner was invited by Ludwig to Hohenschwangau, where he conjured up the most marvellous things for the King. In the mornings Wagnerian motifs resounded from the turrets of the castle, the *Königsgruß* (royal greeting) and the *Gralsgruß* (greeting of the Holy Grail) were performed by the oboists of the First Infantry regiment (Wagner was able to issue these orders). Ludwig was so enchanted that another twenty musicians had to come to enable his guest to give concerts in the evenings. During the day they drove out in a four-horse carriage; the weather was unusually mild and sunny. They revelled in the joys of the countryside and in lofty conversation; on returning home, the square piano provided new ecstasies. Ludwig arranged

a firework display for the last evening – but Wagner also had a surprise in store: 'Lohengrin's Arrival'. A shimmering figure emerged from the mist on the Alpsee. The adjutant general Fürst Paul von Thurn und Taxis, dressed as Lohengrin, stood in a boat pulled by a small skiff covered by a wooden swan. Ludwig commanded a repeat performance two days later. In his recollections he cast himself in the rôle of the Swan-knight, however, and Professor A. Gwala-Trill lent the Swan-knight Ludwig's features in his painting *(above)*.

Opposite page:
The royal Swan-knight
in the Blue Grotto
at Linderhof.
Taken from a contemporary
picture card.

König Ludwig II.
In der blauen Grotte zu Linderhof.

The square piano on which Richard Wagner played at Hohenschwangau.

Wagner in exile in Switzerland. Grey and wasted, he recalls the luxury of his Munich home; he is not yet able to believe his fall from the celestial heights. In Munich his enemies are triumphant.

Scene change –
the Favourite falls

Even before Wagner visited the King, Pfistermeister had openly declared war. He had received explicit orders from Ludwig to grant the favourite a new loan of 40000 gulden. Had there ever been other strangers who did nothing but run up debts, denying themselves no luxuries at the expense of the Cabinet? Pfistermeister arranged a childish trick together with the cashier: when Cosima went to collect the money she discovered it was in sacks of small coins. Cosima, "that red-headed lady", did not bat an eyelid and called a cab, signed the receipt and drove back to the Briennerstrasse – her bold profile in the air and the sacks around her. Wagner had attempted in Hohenschwangau to persuade Ludwig to get rid of Pfistermeister, and the Cabinet was attacked in a newspaper article inspired by Wagner – but Pfistermeister hit back immediately, letting it be known in a reply that Wagner had cost the Treasury 190000 gulden in less than a year. This happened while Wagner was once more in Munich, and he demanded that the King dismiss Pfistermeister for "patriotic reasons". This letter offended Ludwig, however, and before he returned to Munich to be harangued by the Court, the Archbishop von Scherr and the whole of the opposition in order to force him to drop Wagner, he had already decided to draw the consequences. The second Cabinet Secretary, Lutz, informed the hated musician that the King wished him to leave Munich.

Wagner burst out into a string of abuse aimed at Pfistermeister, but Lutz cut him short with the words: "Control yourself; I am here in my official capacity!" This expulsion seemed so outrageous to Wagner that it required a letter from Ludwig to make him go. On 10th December 1865 he boarded a train for Switzerland, accompanied only by his old dog and his Bohemian servant, Franz. He looked pale and confused. Cosima, who still bore the name 'von Bülow' brought him to the station.

1866 – Civil War

1866 saw the end of the crinoline *(right)* which had dominated ladies' fashions since 1854. It had been the object of much laughter – and still, now it was to disappear, many spoke of it being the end of the 'good old days'. And they were not quite so wrong, as we will see. Bismarck's aim was the exclusion of Austria from the German Confederation. He tried to tempt the Bavarian Minister-President von der Pfordten with the prospect of two spheres of influence: one Prussian, one Bavarian in the south. But the conservative politician refused point-blank to further this plan, and Ludwig agreed. He was convinced that "the Prussians would want even more later". Shortly before this, on 7th May, the democrat Cohen-Blind attempted to assassinate Bismark Unter den Linden *(below)*, unsuccessfully, however. His victim, "the most hated man in Prussia", had the presence of mind to disarm the would-be assassin. Bismarck continued on as if nothing had happened...

We're off to fight the Prussians! Departure of the militia.

↑ 1 8 6 6 ↑

Defeat

Ludwig, who wished to avoid war at all costs, signed the order for mobilization on 10th May, and toyed for the first time with the idea of abdication. On 22nd May, Wagner's birthday, he was meant to open the *Landtag* (Diet) – but he escaped to Triebschen in Switzerland, to Wagner. The journey became known and was extremely badly received. The King did make his Speech from the Throne at the postponed opening of the *Landtag* on 27th May and then, contrary to all expectations, withdrew to Berg – now was the time every-

one would have liked to have seen him in the capital. Prior to an outing to the Roseninsel *(opposite page)* Pfistermeister reported the troops were on the march.

"If the Prussians only knew they were going to die tomorrow..." sang the Bavarian troops when the King visited them in Franconia. His presence cast a spell over the men. A Hessian battalion commander reported: "...a youth entered in a blue and silver uniform with a pleated riding cloak around his shoulders, like a Knight of the Grail with his wonderfully dark, shining eyes; he was so beautiful, with a beauty of the other world, that my heart almost stopped. I whispered to my Bavarian neighbour who, like all the Bavarians present, had risen on his entrance, 'Who's that?' 'Our young King,' he replied." Ludwig, who had little idea of military matters, refused to command the troops. He returned home and let off fireworks every evening on the *Roseninsel* in Lake Starnberg... It was not until 3rd July, when the Austrian army was defeated at Königgrätz, that the Southern Germans met the Prussians. The war was lost after a few weeks despite the fact that the Bavarians, as the Prussian General Manteuffel admitted, had fought "like lions".

The Queen Mother, Marie, visits and administers to the wounded.

The Württemberg artillery in battle at Tauberbischofsheim.

Siegesjubel
in Berlin

Victory Celebrations in Berlin

The Bavarians numbly received the news of this turning-point in history, the increase in Prussia's power. In Berlin, however, 55 daughters of the city greeted the victorious army with their King. The young women wore white gowns with golden belts, green wreaths in their hair and black and white bows on the left shoulder. The beautiful young lady carrying the scroll was Henriette Gabler. The poem she read to the King ended with the words: "God was and will be on Your side – until palms wave over the laurels!" What this referred to remained the secret of the poet, Christian Friedrich Scherenberg. The young women then presented their laurel wreaths on cushions and Berlin celebrated for three days and nights – with parades, speeches and cheers.

Cabinet Reshuffle

The Bavarian Commander-in-Chief, Prince Karl, and Ludwig von der Tann were considered "traitors"; in fact, this was the requital for an unmilitary dynasty, and whipping boys had to be found; one of these was the Minister-President von der Pfordten. This extremely competent politician was also forced to bring home Bismarck's peace terms: concession of two districts to Prussia, 30 million gulden indemnity and a secret agreement for mutual support. This was political death for Pfordten, who had enjoyed almost unlimited power in Bavarian politics. His successor was Fürst Chlodwig zu Hohenlohe-Schillingsfürst. Lutz also had to go, as well as Pfistermeister, who was replaced by the noble Privy Councillor von Neumayr.

Left: The dismissed Minister-President von der Pfordten.

Below left:
Privy Councillor von Neumayr, Pfistermeister's successor.

Below: Chlodwig von Hohenlohe-Schillingsfürst, later sent to Paris as the German ambassador by Bismarck.

Empress Elisabeth of Austria

...and her sister Sophie

A Triumphal Tour and an Unexpected Betrothal

Ludwig could not be persuaded to welcome the returning army. He just as stubbornly rejected a proposal by his ministers that he make a tour of his land. Within the royal family the question of a change in monarch was seriously discussed. Ludwig himself felt that he was a 'mock' King and once more considered abdicating. Wagner, in whom he confided, was angry with Ludwig and threatened to break with him completely. This shook the King and on 10th November 1866 with a retinue more than one hundred strong he toured the provinces ravaged by the war. The tour became a triumphal journey. He was heralded in Bayreuth, Kissingen, Aschaffenburg and Würzburg. He visited the battlefields and the destroyed villages, he decorated the graves of soldiers, awarded campaign medals and played the role of the beneficient monarch. Finally he arrived in Nurem-

berg, where he held receptions, visited the working masses of Fürth, danced with the radiant daughters of the 'Bürger' and was simply idolised.

Then, early in 1867, there was a court ball in Munich at which he paid the most conspicuous of attentions to his cousin Sophie. The next day, 22nd January, witnessed the announcement of his engagement to her. This took everyone by surprise, including Herzog Max, his fiancée's father. A week later, after an officers' ball, he declared that although there had been beautiful ladies there, his cousin Sophie had outshone them all. However, it was soon being said quite openly in Court circles that the King had literally "stumbled" into the engagement, and that it was becoming increasingly difficult from day to day for the royal bridegroom to picture himself as a husband.

In Paris

Ludwig's abdication plans resulted from his extremely delicate sense of honour. His land had been conquered and he saw himself as a 'mock' King, before him the example of his grandfather Ludwig I, who had retired from the field virtually without a fight. Only Richard Wagner, well aware of the privileges which he owed to a reigning Maecenas, was able to dissuade him from abdicating. As to the betrothal, no-one was more surprised than the royal bridegroom himself, and he hurriedly departed for the World Exhibition in Paris. Although the city was swarming with reigning heads of state, Napoleon III spared much time for Ludwig, who spoke very good French. He showed him romantic castles, gave dinners – and warned the Bavarian King against the Prussians. Ludwig visited the theatre almost every evening, ran an admiring and expert eye over thoroughbreds in the Bois de Boulogne *(below)* and devoted his attention to the art treasures of the World Exhibition. The highlight of the Exhibition, however, was a 'machine for lifting persons' as the first lift was elaborately termed *(right)*. This construction heralded the dawn of the industrial age – by comparison, Ludwig inhabited an unreal, medieval dream world.

The first lift as exhibited at the World Exhibition in Paris.

Society meets in the Bois de Boulogne.

45

Zur Vermählung Jhrer Majestäten

KÖNIGS LUDWIG II. UND KÖNIGIN SOPHIE VON BAYERN.

Dem bayerischen Volke gewidmet

46

When is the Wedding?

First the wedding was set for 25th August, Ludwig's birthday, and then for 12th October, the day on which both Ludwig I and Maximilian II had married. In the meantime Emperor Napoleon passed through on a journey with the Empress Eugénie, and Ludwig presented his bride to them. Eugénie, whose elegance set the tone in Europe, looked with surprise at the beautiful Sophie – and suddenly embraced her in a movement that was curiously effusive, almost maternal. Sophie was to think back often to this gesture, for Ludwig's behaviour became increasingly strange. He had made her precious gifts but had then disappeared to study the Minstrels' Hall at Wartburg castle. That was followed by the trip to Paris, and now the wedding date had been postponed again to 12th November. Between confused letters the bride received flowers, often in the middle of the night, and Ludwig appeared with the royal crown, which Sophie was made to try on. This scene led her to say tearfully, "He does not love me, he is merely playing with me". But at the Residenz rooms were being equipped for her, and a magnificent wedding carriage stood ready...

Pictures of the bride and groom were everywhere to be seen. A print commemorating the forthcoming marriage appeared (*opposite page*), a coin was minted (*below*), and every album now included a portrait taken by the court photographer. But this photograph in particular (*right*) increasingly prompted one thought – that the couple did not give the appearance of being suited for a life together. When, at a ball given in honour of the couple by Prince Hohenlohe, the King left at 10 o'clock to see the final act of a play, the sceptics had to be believed when they whispered, "The marriage won't take place".

A Frank Word

Herzog Max was one of the most popular men in Munich. Both his palace on the Ludwigstrasse and his country seat in Possenhofen were scenes of conviviality and social intercourse. The main reason for his popularity was his love of the zither, which he played expertly *(left)*. Four of his daughters had made brilliant matches. Elisabeth, the second and most beautiful daughter, had become Empress of Austria and now such a malheur had befallen the youngest. Ludwig was merely manipulating her and that was unacceptable. Furious, the Duke wrote to her odd suitor saying that by no means did he wish to force Sophie upon him but he must humbly request Ludwig to say "yes" or to withdraw his offer of marriage. He only visited Sophie once a fortnight, anyway, although Possenhofen was no distance from Schloss Berg on the opposite side of the lake, and the constant postponement of the wedding was damaging to Sophie's honour.

A Row at the Residenz

Ludwig was beside himself with rage when Max, the bride's father, demanded a final decision. A bust of Sophie, which had been standing on his desk, was hurled into the courtyard and lay there in pieces – a clear indication to the whole court of the break between the couple. The wedding carriage *(right)*, which had cost over a million crowns and which had already been on a "trial run" through the city, ended up in an outbuilding. The final words which Ludwig addressed to poor Sophie in a farewell note were; "Your cruel father is tearing us apart!". For months on end the King's name was not mentioned in the Herzog's household, and even the "Dove" Elisabeth was angry at her fickle and unpredictable "Eagle".

The Fate of the Spurned Bride

Without hesitation and without a courteous period of reflection, Ludwig broke off his engagement. The break was received with equanimity. It had been expected, and many had been troubled by the close blood ties between Ludwig and Sophie. Only the rural population was deeply disappointed. Their sense of propriety was offended by the 'bachelor' state of their King.

Whenever peasants came up to the city, the 'Augustinerbräu' *(above)* and other taverns frequented by them were scenes of heated arguments. Much worse, Sophie became the target of foolish gossip. It was alleged that the King had caught her boxing the ears of a chambermaid, that he had seen her secretly meeting the court photographer... – in short, all blame was put on her. She endured such treatment

and barely a year later married the Herzog of Alençon. Eyewitnesses reported that, at the altar, her "I do" sounded as though she meant "I don't mind" or "For all I care". At the wedding breakfast the 'Brautchor' from Lohengrin was played. Hearing it must have given rise to strange feelings in Sophie, for once she had exercised great diplomacy in befriending Wagner in order to gain the goodwill of her powerful rival. Ludwig did everything possible to destroy all traces of the planned marriage. The coins were withdrawn from circulation, commemorative prints were bought up and acid was poured onto the copper plates and lithographic blocks. All prints made of a portrait describing Sophie as "Queen of Bavaria" were burnt in Ludwig's presence. But one copy survived and is reproduced on page 51.

Sophie never became the "Queen of Bavaria" and it is open to conjecture whether she was happy in her marriage to the Herzog of Alençon. In May 1897 she met a horrible death in a fire at a charity bazaar in Paris (below). "She insisted heroically that the young girls be saved first", reported an eyewitness.

SOPHIE
KOENIGIN VON BAYERN.

Women and the King...

"Such a handsome look has our dear King"

(comment by an old fruit seller from Starnberg who once saw Ludwig ride by)

Many a female imagination buzzed with thoughts of the handsome, enigmatic King. Women were simply obsessed with the idea of seeing him, if only once, or failing that, of acquiring a picture of him in his coronation regalia or as Grand Master of the Order of the Knights of St. George. Some matrons of good family, however, would stalk the Residenz corridors with their daughters in the hope that not only would they cross paths with the King, but that he, hopelessly bewitched, would also sweep up their pretty little daughters into his arms. The King's bodyguards uttered monstrous oaths, cursing the stupidity and audacity of the women, for some no sooner had they been ejected would return through the next gate. Only the singers of the Court Theatre had free access, and they were most graciously invited to private recitals. This caused some to entertain quite exaggerated hopes, whereupon they possibly grew too bold and were never invited again. Three favourites did hold sway for a considerable period. Marie Dahn-Hausmann *(left)* was very close to Ludwig. He had been very impressed with her as Thekla (Wallenstein) while he was still Crown Prince and had since presented her with many tokens of his esteem. Their relationship was almost a family one, for she was happily married and was almost a substitute mother. Nevertheless she adored him and was immeasurably happy that Ludwig always stressed the "affinity of spirit" that linked them.

"Let me look into your shining eyes and then welcome death"

(from a letter by a high-born admirer)

The portrait of the singer Josefine Scheffsky *(above)* is very flattering for in reality, apart from having Brunhilde proportions, she also had an exceedingly common face – Ludwig only allowed her to sing in his winter garden if she hid behind a screen of foliage. However, he was rather fond of gossip and she was an excellent source. When providing gossip she was even allowed to sit opposite him. She made the mistake, however, of once maligning Bürkel *(right)*, the *Hofrat,* and this proved to be her downfall. He knew that she had made Ludwig a "gift" of a carpet and had demanded 1500 Marks from cabinet funds to pay for it. Although such reimbursement was indeed usual in such cases, she had in fact paid only 300 marks for the carpet and had deceived Ludwig into believing that it came from an Indian prince. The *Hofrat,* who had always thought her tale a little unlikely, now took it upon himself to discover the truth of the matter. As the lady had bought the carpet from his brother-in-law Rosipal, the game was soon up. Nothing made Ludwig more angry than self-interest. She was immediately dismissed and stripped of her title of *'Kammersängerin'.* It was a hard punishment. Notwithstanding this, the newspapers also ran scornful commentaries on the carpet incident and it provided the people of Munich with a spicy and amusing topic of conservation. Such comic incidents involving the King were unusual, more usual were episodes such as the "Wagner case" which darkened the popular mood. And this case was of far greater concern to Bürkel too.

awake at nights, and suddenly he laid his head on her bare shoulder – only to have her push him away without uttering a word. Later she would relate this story with such genuine regret in her voice that it seems unlikely she invented the incident. It is clear that Lila lacked a great deal of the vivacity attributed to Hungarian women, and was more concerned about not creasing her dress. On another occasion in the rain-dewed garden she fretted about her expensive shoes, and when Ludwig wanted to present her with a freshly picked posy she made a fuss about her gloves. "You will receive the flowers in another form", he said with a smile, and sent them to her pressed in a velvet frame. "What a despicable thing!" were her very words, she having expected the flowers to be set in diamonds. Then suddenly it was all over. In Ludwig's eyes she had become "that Bulyowsky hussy", as he had discovered that she had been using his name to obtain the best castings. However, his adoration for Elisabeth *(below)* far surpassed any of his dalliances. He, the gentle dreamer, was no match for her. She possessed courage and energy, and whilst he always sought refuge in his sense of majesty, she had the power to detach herself from courtly life and was a 'liberated woman' well ahead of her time.

Lila von Bulyowsky

She might have become the "Bavarian Pompadour". This pretty Hungarian was a talented actress who, in her spectacular role as 'Maria Stuart' *(opposite page)*, once moved the King so much that the *Allerheiligenhofkirche* had to be opened after the performance so that he could pray for the ill-fated queen doomed to execution. He then had Heigl, the court painter, immediately paint Lila von Bulyowsky as 'Maria Stuart', and when she visited Hohenschwangau, incidents took place which could have won her everything. At all events Ludwig once confessed to her that no woman had yet belonged to him. They sat next to each other on his bed reciting 'Egmont' (such was the King's memory that he knew all the parts of his favourite pieces by heart and often used to correct actors on stage). It was a situation hundreds of women yearned for, but Miss Bulyowsky remained impassive. He even went on to tell her that his passion for her kept him

Renewal of the Friendship with Wagner

The 21st June 1868 was a day of triumph for Richard Wagner. He had on frequent occasions been in Munich but had been careful not to attract attention. He had wanted to sit unnoticed in the theatre during the première of 'The Mastersingers', but Ludwig seated him at his side in the royal box. This was an unprecedented mark of favour and the opera was a tremendous success. "Wagner, Wagner!", the audience shouted enthusiastically, and at Ludwig's behest Wagner took a bow in the royal box, retaining his composure only with great difficulty. It was at this time that various intrigues led to Semper falling greatly out of favour with the King. He was to have built the *Festspielhaus*, and this finally put paid to the project. However, Ludwig had lost the most talented architect of his time.

Above left: Richard Wagner, from a portrait by Lenbach.

Above right: The hapless architect Gottfried Semper, treated with contempt for years.

Left: The King, his mother and Prince Otto in the country residence of Elbigenalp.

From the time his engagement was broken off Ludwig led a secluded bachelor's life at Schloss Berg. The appartments were badly furnished and disorder reigned everywhere, but he was unperturbed by this. Great heaps of books were brought from the state library and he would spend whole nights reading, unless he happened to be out on interminable moonlight rides or a Wagner singer had been sent for. He managed to regain his self-control for state occasions, and even attended the merchants' balls and the traditional rustic ceremony of the "Metzgersprung" *(below)*. Only the newly founded Munich Sports Club of 1860 instilled an indomitable distrust in him, although he himself was an excellent swimmer and the possibility that the club gymnasts might be anarchists inimical to the state had long been discounted. The political event of the period: Hohenlohe sealed the alliance with Prussia – albeit with Ludwig's reluctant approval. However, he considered Wagner's breach of confidence an even greater humiliation than Bavaria's lost independence. Shortly after 'The Mastersingers' he came into possession of irrefutable evidence of Wagner's association with Cosima. Although correspondence was eventually resumed, Ludwig kept his vow not to see Wagner for many years.

Flight from Reality

August 1868 brought a new meeting with the Russian Tsar and Tsarina in Bad Kissingen, and when Maria Alexandrovna of Russia *(opposite page, above left)* also visited Munich, she accepted Ludwig's invitation to visit Schloss Berg. His ship "Tristan" *(opposite page, above right)* carried her and her entourage off to the Roseninsel where Ludwig held a magnificent banquet with a fireworks display *(opposite page, below)* in a magical array of colours. The lavishness of the tables and all the entertainments were reminiscent of the legendary banquets held at the court of Louis XIV, the Sun King. In that same year Ludwig's admiration for the absolute monarchy of that king began to take concrete form with the construction of Linderhof Palace. On repeated occasions he had visited Trausnitz Castle in Landshut *(right)* and had had some of the appartments refurbished. The result was an uninspiring decoration in the new German renaissance style. This was by no means a rehearsal for the reckless building mania that was to become part of his life-style. In the peaceful Graswang valley a construction began to emerge which, amidst the rugged mountain scenery, bore all the splendour of a castle in the French style. Work could hardly proceed fast enough for the royal builder, and that at a time when the railway terminated at Weilheim and the only available method of transporting the building materials was by horse-drawn wagon.

Below: The foundation stone was laid on 5th September 1869 and the building work was completed in scarcely six years.

Hothouse Dreams

The winter garden in the Munich *Residenz* acquired its true exotic splendour in 1874. Ludwig used to spend entire nights there, and it was in this hothouse that many of his dreams mellowed. For example, he suddenly decided to visit Versailles – an idea which Bismarck, amongst others, considered "highly regrettable", but he nevertheless went on to make the preparations for the visit. Ludwig, in the guise of the 'Graf von Berg', departed with Holnstein and four servants on 20th August 1874, and on 25th August, his birthday and name-day, the French government had the 'Grandes Eaux' of Versailles play for him – at a cost of 50 000 francs to the state treasury. This incensed the press, but the newspaper 'Figaro' wrote on a conciliatory note, "He is not a wicked king ... he has never even accompanied his soldiers, apart from on the piano". To the astonishment of his guides Ludwig knew the Palace of Versailles better than they did, and no demonstrations marked his stay. Only a couple of street urchins who followed the King mimicking his peculiar stiff gait had to be chased away. Then in 1875 there followed a brief visit to Rheims.

Fantastic tales were told of the idyllic 'Tusculum' which the King had had constructed on the roof of the Residenz. Few were allowed access to it, and there were even high-ranking dignitaries who disguised themselves as gardeners or electricians to satisfy their curiosity. In the sultry hothouse air grew palms, laurels and cypresses, between which flew

*Right: Postcard showing the King
dreaming in the barge
of the winter garden.*

König Ludwig II. im Wintergarten der Residenz in München.

humming-birds and parrots swung, often frightening the staff, as they could convincingly mimic the King's loud laugh. The King should not be thought of as one who was constantly serious or always wantonly daydreaming. He had a laugh which could suddenly turn into one of scornful mockery. Light from the royal tent glowed on the bank of a small lake, upon which a barge was moored and swans glided. A system of lights could produce enchanting effects in all colours. An artificial moon shone from the domed glass roof and an ingenious pasteboard landscape could make the Himalayas rise up. What went on in this sultry world of theatrical sets was once described as follows in a 'penny dreadful' entitled "The Private Life of the King": "The lady singers' ideals were different from those of the King. One constantly tried to make advances, but to no avail. Once in the King's winter garden, when she thought she and the King to be alone, she fell as if by accident into the artificial lake and cried for help, assuming the King would be gallant enough to come to her rescue. However, this was not the case. The King, with complete indifference, simply rang for a servant and had him help the lady out of the water". A drawing *(below right)* captures this memorable moment. Reports and 'revelations' of this nature were eagerly read. Although much of the material was fabricated, every word was believed. The barge is now on display in the 'König Ludwig Museum' in Schloss Herrenchiemsee *(below left)* and is the last remnant of the gigantic hothouse which caused such a strain on the structure of the old walls of the Residenz. When they toppled during the last war, the heavy lead plates could be seen amongst the heap of rubble, these once having sealed the floor of the artificial lake to prevent seepage into the rooms below.

The lively fantasies of the people of Munich were so captured by the idea of Ludwig's winter garden that they were always ready to believe the most amazing rumours that circulated in this connection.

Scene aus dem kgl. Wintergarten.

Elisabeth Ney

The only statue of the King *(above right)* sculpted from life is the work of Elisabeth Ney *(above left, painting by Friedrich Kaulbach)*. She was one of the most remarkable female characters of her time. As she later went to America, where a Ney Museum is dedicated to her in Austin, Texas, she is always thought of as having been an American. She was, however, born the daughter of a sculptor in Munich in 1833, and was also the great-niece of Marshal Ney. She was extremely beautiful, hard-headed and eccentric, and throughout her life kept her marriage to the Scottish doctor Montgomery a secret. The couple therefore often caused scandal, to which she was quite indifferent, but her husband should be admired for his unfailing patience. Gottfried Keller who, like many others, was hopelessly enraptured by her, immortalized her in the fourth volume of "Der Grüne Heinrich" by modelling the character of the 'Grafentochter' on her. Schopenhauer honoured her with his friendship, and in 1867 Ludwig II had a house built for her in Munich. In 1868 he consented to sit for her. However, he did express to others his "greatest displeasure" at her having taken the liberty of measuring his head with a ruler and compass. During the sittings his head of cabinet, Lipowsky, had to read from "Iphigenia". When Ludwig wanted to present her with jewels she curtly declined, expressing a preference for flowers, which she indeed received. In 1870 she left with her husband for Texas to found a 'model colony'. This ambitious project failed, costing her the international fame of which she would otherwise have been assured. She died a highly respected woman in Austin in 1907, but at heart she was very lonely and unhappy.

The Passing of King Ludwig I

The King, whose intellect was still fully alert, died on 28th February 1868 in Nice in his 82nd year. His passing meant the departure of one of Europe's most gallant gentlemen, a scintillating wit who loved life and who was hopelessly charmed by beautiful women. Even though he did abdicate, he nevertheless constantly strove to protect Bavaria's cause and the royal dignity of his grandson. He more than once gave him invaluable advice. In return he won touching affection from Ludwig II, who showed an awesome respect for this worldly-wise old man whose artistic inclinations he shared to a great extent. But although the deceased king had had to come to terms with unalterable facts, he became increasingly less able to penetrate the wall of shyness and mistrust behind which his grandson hid himself.

Right: Marie, the Queen Mother. Photo circa 1868.

Below: King Ludwig I of Bavaria in old age; painting by Franz von Lenbach. He was a familiar figure in Munich, and had long been forgiven for Lola.

The Queen Mother

She had long lost all influence and almost all contact with her son. With her unassuming nature and her simple intellect, which was totally devoid of artistic interests, she was unable to establish any rapport with him while Ludwig, who in his childhood had loved her dearly, gradually drifted further and further apart from her. The more perceptive regarded her insignificant and naive personality to be an indisputable sign of the dangerous consequences of concentrated inbreeding. Her immediate ancestors included undisputed psychopaths, and even if she herself was sound, considerable negative factors must have been passed down from her side into the blood of the Wittelsbach princes. Her whole life long she would make excuses for her son, her main exoneration for him being that his father had died when he was still so young. She felt most at ease on carefree, intimate occasions. The pleasure she showed when in her younger days she had buttered bread for all and sundry on court outings she likewise displayed in her later years while sitting among the regular patrons of Munich's 'Hofbräuhaus' who affectionately knew her as 'Maari'. In her pocket she always carried beer-tokens, which could be exchanged for a litre of beer and which she freely distributed. Her "ecstatic longing for death" was fulfilled on 17th May 1889. On two occasions she had said aloud, "I ask forgiveness of all those whom I have ever wronged", adding with great sincerity, "I thank all those who have ever showed me kindness".

Crucifixion Group in Oberammergau. Following a visit to the passion plays King Ludwig II commissioned this stone sculpture by Halbig, which he presented to the town. The twelve-metre-high group was, in compliance with his wishes, erected on the Friedenshügel.

Neuschwanstein

The white wonder atop a craggy peak by the rushing waters of the Pöllat was planned by the King (at the same time as Linderhof) to reproduce the legendary "Sängersaal" or Minstrels' Hall of Wartburg. The theatre designer Jank produced two sketches, a castle courtyard (*opposite page, above*) and a facade (*below*), upon which the final designs were based. The castle was to tower above Hohenschwangau like an aery. In the presence of the King the foundation stone of Untersberg marble was laid in the 'palas' of the castle on 5th September 1869. During construction the castle was subjected to many a modification as Ludwig tended away from the romantic and towards the religious, towards his 'grail'. A masterpiece at that time was the construction of the road and water supply up to the castle. Firstly the gate-house was built; this accommodated the King's rooms on the second floor. The living quarters were decked with murals by Wilhelm Hauschild and depicted "the medieval age of chivalry" (*below right*). From here the King would watch the progress of the 'palas'. To reach this room Ludwig had to leave the corner tower of the gate and cross a flat roof (*below left*). It was 1873 before the walls of the castle were built (*right*). However, the politics of the real world encroached on Ludwig's unreal world. On 13th July 1870 Bismarck's 'Ems telegram' shattered the peaceful heavens.

The Bliss of the Moment: Ludwig at a Knighting Ceremony. As grand master of the Order of the Knights of St. George the King touches the shoulders of a vassal with an ancient, mighty sword. The water-colour, attributed to Friedrich Eibner, depicts a medieval ceremony which Ludwig performed with inimitable dignity (left). The age of chivalry was reborn. Such gatherings were the fulfilment of his dreams and he loved to participate in them.

Right: Sketch by Christian Jank for the medieval castle at Falkenstein.

1870 – A Promise kept

On 15th July 1870, the day on which France declared war on Prussia, Ludwig hurried from Linderhof to Berg. Cabinet Secretary Eisenhart explained the situation and consultations lasted from 11 p.m. until 3 a.m. the next morning. During this time Eisenhart was not permitted to sit. A peaceful solution was not possible, the answer was to side with Prussia in war. But this meant allowing all decisions, even concerning the peace treaty after war, to be removed from Ludwig's hands – tantamount to relinquishing the crown. Hours passed before Ludwig finally uttered the words, "Yes, we shall ally ourselves with Prussia". When Eisenhart returned at 6 a.m. he found the King lying on his blue-silk 'bed of Heaven', his eyes radiant. Elated by the satisfaction of honouring a promise, he declared with royal pride, *"Bis dat qui cito dat"* (he gives twice who gives quickly). Eisenhart received orders to mobilize the army and by the time Graf Bray and Freiherr von Pranckh arrived in the afternoon, this was well under way. According to the terms of the alliance the army was reorganized along Prussian lines – all citizens were liable for military service, no-one was exempt. On 27th July the Prussian Crown Prince Friedrich arrived in Munich as Commander of the Southern Armies. To the surprise of the Munich inhabitants the black, white and red flag of the North German Confederation was hoisted in the city for the first time. Ludwig had been reluctant to permit this, but had behaved politely in accompanying his guest to the Residenz.

The King in Bavarian General's uniform.

Bavarian War Minister Freiherr von Pranckh.

Foreign Minister Graf Bray.

A Storm of National Fervour

On 27th July the Residenz was at the centre of tumultuous scenes *(below)*. In the *Hoftheater* over 2000 people awaited the gala performance of 'Wallensteins Lager'. This was preceded by a prolog written and read by the young actor Ernst Possart *(left)*. Theatre director von Perfall had commissioned him to do this as none of the Munich poets had been able to adapt quickly enough to the Prussian accent. Possart flattered both dynasties – he portrayed the German nation as being led by a kingly pair, the Bavarian lion and the Prussian eagle. It was pompous and as the lines: "Der König rief, mag denn das Schicksal walten, ich will dem Bundesgenossen Treue halten" were read, Ludwig made as to embrace the Prussian Crown Prince. The jubilation of the crowds knew no bounds. Possart wrote later: "As the two legendary figures, the tall, blond-bearded, nordic King's son with the flashing blue eyes, and the still taller, dark-haired Bavarian ruler embraced, wave after wave of unabating applause was heard. For minutes I could not continue". But continue he did, heightening the pathos until the officers in the theatre rattled their sabres. From the King Possart received a life-size half-length portrait. Even the Prussian Crown Prince was satisfied with him and remarked to his staff officer: "He gave a very decent performance there".

Bavaria and Prussia on the same Side

The offensive of the Third German Army under the command of Crown Prince Friedrich was designed to give Bavarians and Prussians alike a common baptism of fire. The Bavarians thus played their part in the first victory on French soil at the battle of Weissenburg. Their commander, who reviewed the troops in Speyer *(opposite page)*, had his opinion that he could rely on his men confirmed in the battle at Wörth *(below)* – and in the storming of Fröschweiler the Second Bavarian Infantry Regiment won its first battle awards. But Sedan was the great test. The French attempted to break out at Bazeille but there stood the Bavarians. Their bravery is shown by their losses, 213 officers and 4000 men. The Sedan campaign resulted in the capture of the Emperor Napoleon III and of 83000 soldiers. The Prussian Crown Prince moved to take up position before Paris whilst von der Tann and the Bavarians embarked on the Loire campaign. In the battle for Orleans von der Tann made amends for 1866 and in the judgement of the Prussians: "The manner in which the Bavarians fought will ensure them everlasting glory". Meanwhile Bismarck wrought his plans concerning the German Emperorship but his proposed meeting between Ludwig and the Prussian King in Versailles never took place. The Bavarian delegates insisted on special privileges and Bismarck made concessions. This gave rise to a violent disagreement between Bismarck and the Prussian Crown Prince who demanded "a show of strength" rather than this "gentle treatment". The fact remains, however, that Ludwig – Monarch of the second largest state – offered the Prussian King the title of Emperor of Germany. And here too, Graf Holnstein played a very special role.

The Kaiserbrief

When describing how this letter originated, it is often stated that Ludwig signed his name to a letter written by Bismarck – it is also often suggested that Graf Holnstein forged the signature. It is true that he pressured the King into writing but, as our copy of the document from the secret Prussian State Archives shows, Ludwig had only 'apparently' copied Bismarck's draft. Ludwig's letter reads: "After Southern Germany's entry to the German Confederation the presidential rights accorded Your Majesty will cover all German States. I have agreed to the unification of the States in the conviction that it is in the interest of the German fatherland and of the allied Princes and in the belief that the rights attaching to the presidential Office of the Confederation in accordance with the constitution will be acknowledged, as a result of the restoration of the German Empire and the Emperorship, as rights which Your Majesty will exercise in the name of the whole German fatherland created by the unification of the States. I have proposed to the German Princes that a joint approach be made to Your Majesty that the exercise of the presidential rights of the Confederation be conjoined with the assumption of the title of Emperor of Germany. As soon as Your Majesty and the allied Princes have informed me of their will, I shall instruct my government to carry out necessary measures to put this agreement into effect". A comparison of both documents shows that Ludwig stressed the proposed "presidential dignity".

46.

König Ludwig II. von Bayern an König Wilhelm I. von Preußen: Anerbieten der Kaiserkrone.

Der Brief ist das Ergebnis langer Bemühungen anderer deutscher Bundesfürsten, insbesondere des Großherzogs Friedrich II. von Baden, und wieder Bismarcks als spiritus rector hinter ihnen. Das ausgeprägte Selbstgefühl Ludwigs II. ertrug es nur schwer, sich einem anderen Fürsten unterzuordnen, dem er sich bisher als ebenbürtig betrachtet hatte. Schließlich ist es nach Abschluß der Verträge mit Bayern, die durch ihre Sonderrechte dem König doch eine bevorzugte Stellung im Deutschen Reiche gewährten, Bismarcks überlegener Diplomatie gelungen, den König nicht nur zur Stellung des Antrages zu bewegen, sondern ihn den Brief sogar nach einem eigenhändigen Entwurf Bismarcks schreiben zu lassen. Der Text dieses Entwurfes lautet:

„Die Erklärungen meiner Minister über den Beitritt Bayerns zum Deutschen Bunde haben meine Bereitwilligkeit dargethan dem Präsidium des Bundes die Rechte zu übertragen, deren Vereinigung in Einer Hand Mir durch die Gesamtinteressen des deutschen Vaterlandes und seiner verbündeten Fürsten geboten schien. Ich habe mich dazu in dem Vertrauen entschlossen, daß die dem Bundespräsidium nach der Verfassung zustehenden Rechte durch Wiederherstellung der deutschen Kaiserwürde als Rechte bezeichnet werden welche Ew. M. im Namen des gesammten deutschen Vaterlandes, auf Grund der Einigung seiner Fürsten ausüben. Ich habe daher meine Regierung beauftragt, bei den verbündeten deutschen Regierungen eine Vereinbarung darüber in Vorschlag zu bringen daß die Ausübung der Präsidial-Rechte des Bundes mit Führung des Titels eines deutschen Kaisers verbunden werde."

Das Schreiben des Königs zeigt geringe, aber doch charakteristische Abweichungen von der Vorlage. In dem Begleitschreiben schob Bismarck, geschickt auf die Psyche des Königs berechnet, in den Vordergrund, daß einmal sonst die Volksvertretung, d. h. der Reichstag, die Initiative in der Kaiserfrage ergreifen werde: „Die Stellung würde gefälscht werden, wenn sie ihren Ursprung nicht der freien und wohlerwogenen Initiative des mächtigsten der dem Bunde beitretenden Fürsten verdankt", dann sei es auch leichter für den König, sich dem kaiserlichen Bundespräsidium unterzuordnen: „Der Deutsche Kaiser ist ihr Landsmann, der König von Preußen ihr Nachbar; nur der deutsche Titel bekundet, daß die damit verbundenen Rechte aus freier Überzeugung deutscher Fürsten und Stämme hervorgehen."

Laut den Kanzleivermerken wurde der Eingang des Schreibens sofort an etliche Bundesfürsten, den preußischen Kronprinzen und Minister Delbrück mitgeteilt, der dasselbe im Reichstag in der Debatte über die Annahme der Verträge zur Kenntnis brachte.

Politisches Archiv des Auswärtigen Amtes. Eigenhändige Ausfertigung.

Left: Bismarck's draft, a diplomatic masterpiece.

Opposite page: Ludwig's 'Kaiserbrief'.

Opposite page, above right: Writing-desk in Hohenschwangau, at which the King wrote this document in Graf Holnstein's presence.

Ludwig signs

Bavaria's Foreign Minister Graf Bray was in favour of a constitutional alliance with the North German Confederation. He influenced the ministers in Munich to exert pressure on the King. And so the first momentous step was initiated by the King's ministers – against a background of nationalistic fervour. Ludwig hesitated and despatched his chief equerry Graf Holnstein to Versailles to "spy out the ground". Holnstein, however, reported immediately to Bismarck and they struck up an immediate understanding. Bismarck insisted on a declaration by Ludwig and the guileless equerry replied: "Your Excellency, you should set down the letter yourself, otherwise there will be difficulties afterwards". Bismarck chuckled and drafted the letter immediately. Four days later Holnstein arrived in Hohenschwangau. Ludwig was in his bed suffering from toothache but Holnstein was insistent and procured the precious document from the King. Ludwig was far from pleased and ordered Holnstein to submit the document to Cabinet Secretary Eisenhart, who also gave his immediate approval. Graf Bray, Foreign Minister and Minister-President and therefore responsible for such matters, was in Munich but was not consulted.

Balloon in which Leon Gambetta escaped from the besieged Paris. He established a national resistance movement, but for which the war would probably have ended in autumn 1870.

Left: Bavarian General von der Tann.

The next morning Holnstein requisitioned a train, such was his haste. This reflects the nature of the 'coup' and Holnstein's adventurous character. It is a gesture befitting him that he noted the name of the train driver on his sleeve so that he could reward him later. When Graf Bray learned of what had happened he was beside himself with rage. He would have asked for territorial concessions. Ludwig's regret is too late. Bismarck praised Holnstein, proposed a toast to His Majesty, the King of Bavaria, and the Prussian Marshall's Office proceeded to send out invitations for the proclamation of the German Emperor at Versailles.

Opposite page, above: Bismarck's quarters in Versailles.

Opposite page, below: Prince Luitpold of Bavaria hands over Ludwig's 'Kaiserbrief' to King Wilhelm of Prussia.

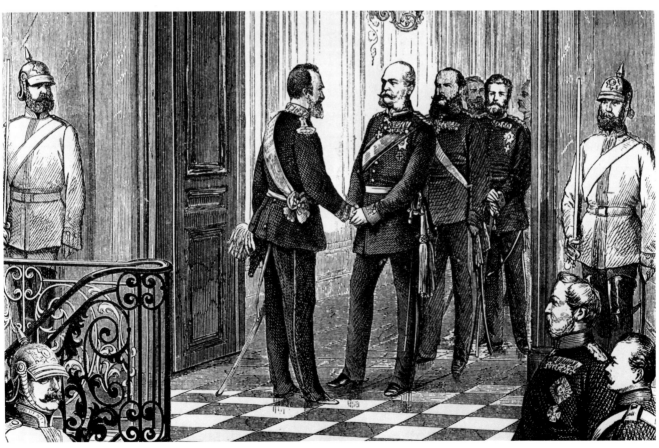

The Proclamation of the German Emperor

The Galerie des Glaces at Versailles was used as a German field hospital *(left)*. It was cleared and, on 18th January 1871, the Hohenzollerns, accompanied by a sea of banners, made their magnificent entrance to proclaim the German Emperor *(below)*. After Bismarck's speech to the 'German nation' the Grossherzog of Baden called for three cheers for the Emperor and a storm of rejoicing erupted. Crown Prince Friedrich Wilhelm found the scene 'greatly moving', Prince Otto of Wittelsbach, unnoticed in the crowd, spoke of 'unutterable woe'.

Opposite page: Contemporary commemorative picture of Ludwig II with a verse by Paul Heyse. Taken from a lithography.

So lang dem Heer das
deutsche Banner weht,
Sei Der geehrt der es zuerst erhöht,
So lang der Bau des Reichs die
Zinne trägt,
Sei Dem gedankt, der treu den Grund gelegt,
Der mit der Krone Zier geschmückt das Dach
Und sprach: dem Kaiser huldigt Wittelsbach.

Heil dem glänz'gen Deutschen Bauens Heil ihm tausendkönig
Ludwig dem edlem Kön'i
Paul Heyse

Ten Days of stormy Debate in the Bavarian Parliament

The Versailles agreement kindled the smouldering anger of the 'patriots party' but it was accepted in parliament by a two-thirds majority – a result mirroring the feeling amongst the populace. Countless citizens had demanded that the parliament give its approval. At that time the King was also known as 'Ludwig the German' – a national commemorative print *(page 79)* took up this theme. The first outward sign of the new situation was the Prussian eagle atop the German Emperor's crown *(above). Above left:* Emperor Wilhelm I. What Emanuel Geibel *(left)* had prophecied two years earlier in a poetic homage to the Prussian King had come true.

Und sei's als letzter Wunsch gesprochen,
Dass noch dereinst Dein Auge sieht,
Wie übers Reich ununterbrochen
Vom Fels zum Meer Dein Adler zieht!

On reading this, Ludwig had promptly discontinued honorary payments allocated by his father Maximilian to the poet. This caused Paul Heyse to renounce his payments. But Ludwig's feelings were apparent – his worries as to Bavaria's future could later be soothed by Bismarck alone. The Chancellor himself displayed towards Ludwig a great liking and understanding in political matters. A picture of Ludwig hung permanently in his study.

16th July, Victory Celebrations

"This is my first ride as a vassal" commented Ludwig bitterly when, after a troop review at the Oberwiesenfeld, in full uniform and "of fairytale appearance", he proceeded to the Ludwigstrasse to review the victorious army in front of the Ludwig I monument. Crown Prince Friedrich headed the troops. Before the university he was greeted by the Lord Mayor and presented a wreath of laurels. His thanks were profuse. The procession, led by generals and staff officers, continued to the Odeonsplatz. There the Crown Prince took his place next to the King and took the salute with him. Flags fluttered, the people rejoiced. The Commander-in-Chief of the victorious sons of Bavaria, the son of the Emperor, beamed, directed his gaze at the troops and revelled in their cheers. The monotonous march of the troops was endless. The Crown Prince raised and lowered his baton without cease, his horse pranced nervously. During the long hours a stony Ludwig sat motionless, as if cast in iron. This was however an example of Bavarian cunning. In view of Ludwig's weight, his horse had been given a morphium injection.

In the evening a gala performance of Paul Heyse's "Der Friede" was held in the *Hoftheater*. Possart had of course composed another prolog but this time he did not have the same success. The Prussian ambassador had read the poem beforehand and had been delighted that the Crown Prince was likened to "Siegfried, the dragon-slayer". He promised the poet the order of the 'Roter Adler'. However Perfall then requested a change as the King was overwrought and Richard Wagner himself had compared the King with Siegfried. Possart was warmly applauded but the Prussian ambassador burst into his dressing-room in a violent rage. "Your manuscript read 'Young Germany's Siegfried' and now you speak of the 'Empire's first knight'. I am discredited and you can cast aside your hopes of an order". The next day brought a further disappointment for Ludwig. He had invited the Crown Prince *(left)* to the Roseninsel and proposed he wear an Uhlan uniform. Friedrich protested he must obtain the Emperor's approval and that he was too corpulent for such a uniform. The King was offended, did not attend the military banquet in the *Glaspalast (above)* that evening and returned to Berg at dawn next day without bidding his guests farewell. Bavaria's future troubled him. In 1874 Emperor Wilhelm I assured him in Munich "that Bavaria need never fear for its independence" and confirmed this in a letter written to Ludwig on the occasion of his birthday on 25th August 1874.

Wagner
in Bayreuth

Above: In 1872 the foundation stone of the Festspielhaus was laid. The official opening of the theatre took place in 1876. Neither event would have been possible, had it not been for Ludwig's generous aid.

Right: Wagner's study in Wahnfried.

The Royal Train

Right: The royal train in blue and gold, with a replica of the King's crown on the roof. Of eight coaches only two, the viewing coach and the salon, whose interior is shown in the illustration below, still exist. The coaches are now the pride of the Nuremberg transport museum. Regilding the coaches cost 30000 DM in present-day currency.

Opposite page: A scene from Richard Wagner's "Walküre, Siegmund's Death".

Shortly after midnight on 6th August 1876 Ludwig was due to arrive in Bayreuth. The town was illuminated, an excited crowd awaited the King. Only Wagner and a few station officials were aware of the King's secret plan. Three quarters of an hour's journey from Bayreuth, at a wayside halt, a state coach waited by the railway track. Wagner, in white waistcoat and black dress-coat, paced up and down impatiently. At half past midnight a signal horn sounded, five coaches approached and screeched to a halt. An aide-de-camp alighted and opened the door of the salon. Ludwig's eyes came to rest on his friend whom he had not seen for eight years but whom he had not forgotten. Wagner clapped his hands to his breast, the tears rolling from his eyes. His outstretched right hand trembled and then was grasped by Ludwig. Both remained silent and those few present exchanged hushed greetings. Amongst them was a Berlin journalist who had brought off the feat of knowing 'where and when' this meeting was to take place. He alone was able to file a report in which he did not fail to mention that Richard Wagner "took a seat next to His Majesty in the royal coach without Ludwig's express invitation".

Neither was he wrong in constating that the King gave signs of a certain surprise, although he countenanced Wagner's behaviour. For several days Ludwig attended the general rehearsals for the 'Ring' and was celebrated rapturously wherever he appeared. When the time came to leave, late in the summer night, torch bearers lined the path to the royal train.

Left: Solemn hours in Wahnfried.
Seated, from the left: Siegfried Wagner, Cosima Wagner and Amalie Materne. Right: Liszt, Cosima's father, at the piano. Fore right: Gräfin Marie Schleinitz and Gräfin Usedom. Standing, left to right: Franz v. Lenbach, Paul Joukorsky, Franz Fischer, Richard Wagner. Seated: Fritz Brand and Hermann Levi. To their right: Hans Richter, Franz Betz and Albert Niemann. In the background, a portrait of the King.

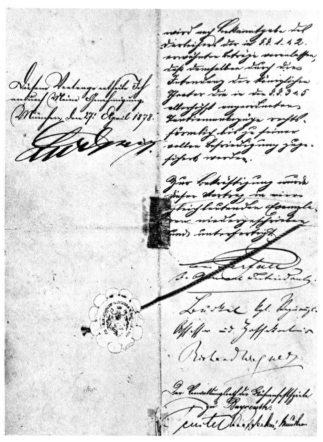

New Debts in Bayreuth and a New Source of Aid

Richard Wagner had found his *Wahnfried* but, in spite of his success, there were still deficits. Again he turned to Ludwig who was unable to offer further aid: the King's building activities had depleted resources so severely. New sources of finance were sought, debts were incurred wherever possible. Von Perfall devised a noble solution. He submitted to the King that for many years the *Hoftheater* had owed its rich artistic development to Wagner's influence and had received significant proceeds, whereas Wagner had received none. He proposed paying Wagner a 10% share of the gross proceeds from his works until the Bayreuth deficit was covered. Ludwig's financial advisor, Bürkel, acquiesced and all was saved.

Opposite page: The Ring of the Nibelung, Walküre.
Set, lithography by Ferdinand Leeke.

Left: The last page of the original eight-page contract dated 31st March 1878, with the signatures of Ludwig, Perfall, Bürkel, Richard Wagner and the administrative advisor to the Bayreuth Festival, the banquier Feustel.

Opposite page: The Ring of the Nibelung, Rheingold,
"Catch the thief! Save the gold!"
Set, fresco by Michael Echter.

Rheingold

The Swimming of the Rhine-Maidens

The audience in the Bayreuth *Festspielhaus* stared mesmerized at the bold faeries of the stage, the like of which they had never seen before. The appearance of Alberichs and the Rhine-Maidens *(opposite page)* was an unprecedented spectacle. How were the effects achieved? Well below the stage *(below)* trolleys with high supports and iron cradles were manoeuvred. These and an iron hoop against which the Rhein-maidens leaned, helped the singers keep their balance. Their robes were drawn back and affixed to give the impression of a mermaid's tail. The trolleys were operated by several men. One cranked the Rhein-Maidens to the height of the stage, another – score in hand – directed the timing of all movements simulating swimming. This complicated contraption was inspected by Paula von Bülow, Mistress of the Robes of the Grossherzog von Mecklenburg-Schwerin. She described it accurately and summarized her impressions such: "It requires strong nerves to sing well in such a precarious position. The orchestra pit was so low that, from various points on stage, it was impossible to see the conductor. Several assistant conductors were posted in the wings to prompt the singers by means of signs or musical cues."

'Separatvorstellungen' at the Hoftheater

"I can have no illusions in the theatre if people constantly stare at me and inspect my every facial movement through their opera glasses. I want to watch and not be watched." Ludwig II once made these observations to Possart. Eventually he asked Perfall if he could be the sole spectator at a rehearsal. This privilege was granted and the famous 'Separatvorstellungen' were born. A total of 208 were held between 6th May 1874 and 12th May 1885. They gave rise to much talk, not least about the large amounts of money wasted by the King. But the *Hoftheater* was a court institution. The people did not pay for it, costs and deficits were covered by the civil list. Moreover, Ludwig alone can be thanked for having Wagner's works performed. Neither should it be forgotten that Perfall, the director, could do as he pleased. The King could not alter the repertory or 'decide' what was suitable for the people. Ludwig's own preference was for historical theatre. His private performances were not secret – the theatre was fully lighted. After the performance Ludwig would often send the actors flowers and presents and would await, in the middle of the night, an immediate letter of thanks.

Above: The stage at the Hoftheater with the curtain closed.

Left: Hoftheater director Freiherr von Perfall.

Right: Karl Heigel, a much-envied author who wrote plays commissioned by Ludwig. These were rehearsed and performed for Ludwig alone. The King's private performances busied several authors writing on themes taken mainly from the Bourbon era.
Absolute realism was essential.

Prince Otto's
Insanity

At the beginning of 1873 signs of mental derangement necessitated the isolation of the once so pleasure-loving Prince Otto *(right).* Since then he had lived under mild restraint in Nymphenburg palace, from whence he escaped on Corpus Christi. He went to Munich and during high mass at the *Frauenkirche* he dashed to the altar steps loudly confessing his terrible sins. A great excitement possessed the congregation but Otto was calmly led away by two ushers. He was taken to Fürstenried castle in order to keep a closer watch on him and to prevent any attempt at suicide. His brother's mental illness aroused deep foreboding in Ludwig ... he feared his own fate. Of late a warm friendship had linked them.

At his behest Otto had been of the party at Versailles and the letter in which he described the proclamation of the Emperor remained imprinted in Ludwig's mind. "Alas, Ludwig" reported Otto, "I can hardly describe the endless sorrow and pain that I felt during the ceremony, how every fibre of my being revolted at everything I saw ... it was all so cold, proud, so brilliant, pompous, ostentatious, heartless and empty ... I felt so constricted and numbed in that hall, outside I could breath again freely." Now the King had lost his last confident for ever. The darkness had closed around him. He neglected state business which, to him, was boring trivia. He was heftily criticised for his castle building, which had now become the sole aim in his life. One day on the way to Linderhof he was startled by a sign 'Abdanken!' *(left)* calling on him to abdicate. At a nod from him the sign was hacked to pieces – but had he himself not entertained such thoughts? He more and more had sought refuge in his royal dignity, creating thereby an ever-wider chasm between himself and his people in order to conceal those moments of darkness which would abruptly befall him.

The Palace of Linderhof

Building work was completed in 1878, the garden in 1877. To Ludwig the palace meant more than outward splendour and he named it 'Meicost-Ettal', not as the uninitiated might suppose, after the nearby Ettal but as an anagram of Louis XIV's boast "L'état, c'est moi". The palace was Ludwig's 'home' where, more than ever, night became day and the King indulged in irreal, twilight dreams. At his lonely dining table, several places were set – in his fantasy Bourbon kings and personnages of their world were his guests. Servants overheard his talks with them and saw how he raised his champagne glass to Marie Antoinette and other beloved images of his fantasy. Below in the vestibule he always raised his hat to the equestrian statue of Louis XIV and lovingly brushed his hand over statuettes, columns and certain trees in the garden.

Above: Equestrian statue of Louis XIV of France in the vestibule; the symbol of the absolute monarchy of the Bourbons.

Left: A dream come true for the dream King: 'Tischlein-deck-dich' in Linderhof.

A Fairy-tale Palace in Golden Splendour

In each room in Linderhof the elaborate ostentation belies the lonliness of the King. The bedroom is in white and gold, a mighty chandelier glitters in the light of over a hundred candles, a precious canopy vaults the wide bed. The sun, whose rays warmed him less and less, shone above his pillow. Ludwig chose the resplendent peacock as his second heraldic animal. The peacock matched the swan in its unsocial ways but was yet shier and more unwelcoming.

Above: The royal bed with a canopy of violet velvet. Panelling with gilded carvings.

Right: Life-size peacock in Sèvres porcelain. West Gobelins room.

In the World of Dreams

The dream world of Linderhof in which the King sequestered himself aroused the curiosity and fantasy of his subjects. Every pictorial representation was gladly received. The painter H. Breling, who had assisted with the decorations, provided some good examples. *Left:* The King in the audience room. *Below:* Ludwig reading in the *Hundingshütte*.

The ash tree with the *Wälsunger* sword, the hearth and chimney, benches, animal skins and primitive tools can all be seen. The King is said to have had drinking bouts here with stable lads, lackeys and *chevauxlegers*. The *Hundingshütte*, a wooden construction, was burned down at the end of the 1945 war.

Richard Wagner's *Hundingshütte* in the *Walküre* was realized by Ludwig in Graswangtal, not far from Linderhof. He often sat there reading books whose content formed a sharp contrast to the primitive surroundings, or else he diverted himself with what were

known as 'living pictures' representing, according to his wishes, a drinking bout in the old Germanic style ... as reported by Luise von Kobell in her book 'König Ludwig II. von Bayern und die Kunst'. The 'Blue Grotto' at Linderhof also served to divert Ludwig: the illuminations required 25 generators. Ludwig sometimes dined in the grotto and invited a guest to join him. His favourite horse was also honoured with a visit to the 'Blue Grotto'...

Following pages:
Left: Linderhof seen from the park.
Right: Audience room.

Right: A caricature: 'King Lohengrin' Realism, malicious distortion and naive idealisation merged in contemporary illustrations.
Below: The King being rowed in the golden cockle-boat in the 'Blue Grotto', an artificial cave. A monumental painting 'Tannhäuser at Venusberg' completes the scene in the magic grotto. When Ludwig tarried there the colours of the set could be changed from red to blue or green.

Es ist eine bitterkalte Winternacht. Der Wald ächzt unter seiner Schneelast, die er kaum mehr zu tragen vermag, sonst herrscht allerwärts die tiefste Stille. Wald und Flur liegen ja in den Banden des Todes. „O Frühlingszeit, wann kommst du wieder, um den Bann zu lösen, wann ist es uns wieder gestattet, alles Leid abzu schüt teln und uns des neugeschenkten Lebens zu freuen!" So mögen die Dryaden träumen, die in den Bäumen wohnen und trauern. „Käme doch eine mächtige Fee, die Alles mit lichtem Glanz erfüllt, daß sie uns wenigstens die Hoffnung brächte, es werde sich Alles wieder zum Guten gestalten.

Horch, was bedeutet dieses Klingen und Schnau ben? Sollte sich der Wunsch der Dryaden so schnell erfüllen? Was naht da in rausender Eile? Fackeln färben den Schnee mit Glut, milchweiße Rosse sprengen heran und eine Fee lenkt sie. Ihr schöner Leib ist von Schilf umrankt, als wäre sie eben erst den Fluthen entstiegen und hoch über ihrem Haupte hält sie eine Krone und von dieser Krone strömt es aus wie Mondlicht. Welcher glückliche Herrscher trägt wohl diese Krone? Hinter der Fee sitzt er, der Mächtige, der Erhabene. Hermelin schmiegt sich um ihn, aus seinem Antlitze aber leuchten Augen, in deren Tiefen eine Zauber- und Märchenwelt zu schlummern scheint.

The Thunder of Hooves

The King's restless nature drove him from castle to mountain hut, from mountain hut to hunting lodge. Holnstein was responsible for the horses, coaches and supplies. Often enough the *Kabinettschef* would follow along and hold forth at the wayside, clothed in his black morning coat, with his blue-velvet portfolio, his speech punctuated by the sound of cow-bells. The King would listen, with gloomy mien, add a few sentences, sign the necessary documents and then the unwelcome admonisher was gone. The normal state carriages were replaced by splendid baroque coaches, as were common at the French court. Munich came to see less and less of its ruler; instead a lively exchange with the country people began. At marriages and at christenings, when turning hay or cutting wood, it would be no surprise to encounter the King talking to the simple people, showing neither shyness nor disdain nor fear of attack. He would talk of harvest prospects and knew many peasants by name. He would address hunters in the forests and young herdsmen might receive a watch as a gift from the King. These are substantiated facts.

Once a year the King would have wooden plank-ing laid over the railway line leading across the Grosshesseloher bridge, which traverses the craggy valley of the Isar at a height of 100 feet and over a distance of almost 300 yards. His sole purpose in doing so was to race across the bridge in a coach, the mountains glittering to the south, the lofty towers of the city rising to the north, below the pounding of horses hooves and the roar of the green waters of the Isar – an incom-parable royal journey as could only have been imagined and put into practice by Ludwig II. In the winter state sleighs would glide through powdery snow and hundreds earned a welcome income clearing miles of pathway of the deep snow.

Opposite page: A sleigh ride by night. Drawing from the newspaper Neues Münchner Tagblatt in 1898 and below the original newspaper report.

Right: From the runners of a magnificent sleigh cherubs rise up bearing a crown which could be illumi-nated by means of a battery under the King's seat. He could switch the lamp in the crown on and off and, by means of a second switch, he could pass horn signals to his outrider.

Below: Ludwig's nymph sleigh.

The King's Restless Nature

Linderhof is in the beautiful Graswangtal, near Ettal, and it was from there that Ludwig II started each winter on his legendary sleigh rides. The dream-like sleigh sped like the wild wind, through the crisp cold of the dark nights by moonlight, on through village, forest and field, up hill and down dale. The border was often crossed, in the Tyrol clandestine accommodation, of which no servant dared make mention, awaited the King. Benumbed stood those fortunate to witness the escort speed by, or those who, awakened by barking dogs, caught a glimpse of this fairy-tale scene.

Left: The King in the heavy fur-coat he wore when journeying by sleigh, a drawing by Professor Hecht.

Left: An autumnal scene. Ludwig ascending the Schachen mountain.

Right: A magnificent sleigh before Linderhof – a journey into the night with six milk-white horses. The dress of the outrider and the piqueurs was of royal splendour – the powdered wigs and three-cornered hats conjured up a rococo scene. The King was seated under fur rugs in the sleigh.

Drawing breath they made the sign of the cross – they knew the lie of the land where gorges and treacherous ponds threatened life and limb. And such journies were made at break-neck speed. On one occasion the outrider lost his way in a blizzard and would have plunged into an abyss had not Hornig, the head groom, intervened at the last second. Ludwig noticed nothing, his head full of dreams of far-off lands over which he held absolute rule. Franz von Löher, Ludwig's archivist, was sent on a voyage of discovery but returned from the Canary Isles, Cyprus, Crete and the Crimea with nothing to suit the King. Later he was to become the target of hostility and ridicule – but he had had a magnificent journey.

Torchlight, silver tinkling of bells – thud of hooves, snorting horses – a sleigh approaches at speed bearing the King in ermine, crown and sceptre in hand. A fairy-tale scene which fades like an apparition into the wintry night . . .

The Moorish room in the Hunting Lodge at Schachen.

Fritz Schwegler, His Majesty's outrider.

The King and his Servants

The Royal Residence on the Schachen was built by Ludwig in 1872. The first floor is a fine illustration of 'oriental' bombast *(left)*. It was here that he had his servants dress in Turkish costume, drink sorbet and smoke hookas – just as he had them quaff mead from drinking horns in the *Hundingshütte* – a diversion they no doubt enjoyed. For his part Ludwig looked on, not without irony. It is reported that, on occasions, he joined in, tested his strength with his servants. He had special favourites whom he heaped with gifts and there were troopers, who having been assigned to service with the King would soon boast brilliant rings on their fingers. Ludwig took great pleasure in making gifts, particularly of rings and watches. Fritz Schwegler *(left)* proudly shows the ring which he received together with a watch and tie-pin from the King. As an outrider he was once called upon to help serve at table. Whilst doing so he was forced to take hold of a fish in his fingers to stop it slipping from the platter. This was noticed by Ludwig but Schwegler made off, afraid of the King's wrath. But, the next day, he received the presents. One of his closest servants was the head groom, Richard Hornig *(below)* who also served him as private secretary before his dismissal in 1885 – he failed to conjure up the millions Ludwig required for his building plans. Hornig was a clever, educated man who had accompanied Ludwig everywhere. He suffered indirectly as a result of the King's hallucinations – the King would imagine a knife in his hand or claim to have heard a gun-shot. Hornig spoke little of such things but he confirmed Ludwig's outbursts of rage, in which insults, threats and blows would rain down on his lackeys.

Head groom Richard Hornig.

Monument of Royalty:
Schloss Herrenchiemsee

In 1873 Ludwig purchased the Herreninsel, an island on Lake Chiemsee, to save its forests from speculation by wood traders. Five years later he began the construction there of his 'Versailles'. To supervise the building work he set up in the old castle (formerly a monastery) and so that he could follow the progress of work from his window, a wide avenue was cleared through the forest. All trees were topped so that using a telescope he had a clear view of the palace site. For Hofrat Düfflip *(right)* who was responsible for the Cabinet Treasury, the prospect of new debts was too much to bear – he resigned.

The room, from which Ludwig II followed the construction of his palace, is the birthplace of modern Germany's constitution.

The Anniversary of Wittelsbach Rule

On the seven-hundredth anniversary of Wittelsbach rule in 1880 the mountain rangers company of the Isarwinkel began celebrations by firing a salute at the grave of those killed in the *Sendlinger Mordweihnacht* in 1705 *(below)*.

The legendary blacksmith of Kochel *(left, painting by Defregger)* and 800 rebellious peasants had then attempted to free Munich from pandour rule. The celebration breathed new life into Bavarian patriotism.

Opposite page: A striking memorial page from the 'Sulzbach Kalender'.

Otto v. Wittelsbach

Friedrich Barbarossa

„Ich weiß mich eins mit meinem treuen Volke,"
  Dieß schöne Wort, das Bayerns König sprach,
Es zittert, — wie der Schein der Morgenwolke
  Im Lenzlaub, — noch in allen Herzen nach
Dieß Wort erst gab die volle, rechte Weihe
  Den Tagen, die so festlich hingerauscht,
Wo Lieb' um Lieb', wo Treue gegen Treue
  Ein ruhmreich Herrscherhaus und Volk getauscht.

Ja, was im Lauf von siebenhundert Jahren
  Als felsenfester Bund sich hat erprobt,
Ob wilde Wetterstürme und Gefahren
  In böser Zeit ihn auch gar oft umtobt;
Das darf die Mit-, das darf die Nachwelt feiern,
  Das, — mögen auch im Wechsellauf der Zeit
Geschlechter um Geschlechter sich erneuern, —
  Das wird besteh'n in Ehren hoch gefeit.

D'rum töne, Harfe, tön' in Jubelweise,
  — Sind auch auf unsern Bergen schon verglüht
Die Freudenfeuer, — tön' zu Ruhm und Preise
  Dem Jubelfeste noch ein Weihelied:
„So lang im Alpschnee und in Himmels Bläue
  „Der Heimath Farben uns entgegen seh'n,
„So lange wird des Bayernvolkes Treue
  „Zum Hause Wittelsbach nicht untergeh'n!

Ernst von Destouches.

1180-1880.

Gedenkblatt
für die Feier des siebenhundertjährigen Regierungs-Jubiläums des Hauses Wittelsbach.

The Island of Roses

Elisabeth, daughter of Herzog Max, Empress of Austria *(opposite page)*, would have been termed a 'devilish woman', were it not for the Habsburg ring on her finger. She was a daring, brilliant rider who mercilessly ran her horses into the ground. She could be cold and scornful but in 1866 she devotedly cared for wounded soldiers during the war. Emperor Franz Joseph never discovered the secret of her soul. She lived in a world of dreams, as did Ludwig, and shared his unworldliness: she spent 46000 gulden a month when travelling.

The enthusiastic friendship between Elisabeth and Ludwig – the 'Dove' and the 'Eagle' as they called each other – lasted for more than two decades. In the centre of the Roseninsel, an island on Lake Starnberg, there stood a small villa *(below left)* and if Elisabeth were staying with her parents in Schloss Possenhofen *(above)*, she would meet Ludwig here in this miniature paradise. Here they were always alone – whatever is recounted of their meetings here is the purest fabrication. Many years later a Gräfin Zanardi-Landi in America claimed to be a child of Ludwig and Elisabeth. But she was unmasked as a prattling pretender – not even able to quote dates to substantiate her fairy-tale.

In the study of the villa stands a writing desk (right) with a secret compartment, into which Elisabeth placed letters if a meeting with Ludwig were not possible. After his death an unopened letter was found. It was marked "From the Dove to the Eagle".

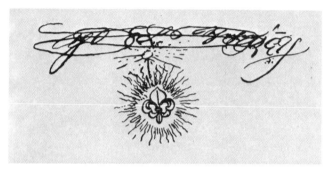

The lines below are Ludwig's authentic entries in his diary. Frequently sentences are broken off unfinished, thus resembling more and more mystic formulae and adjurations.

Nicht August, nicht September mehr, nicht Oktober
Heute Lilien – Kuß, v. Königs-Lippen
letzter! – Schachen …

Doch in dem Herzen deines Volkes wird's
Wie Oel im Feuer, entzünden eine Brunst,
Die all' des Feindes Werk verzehrt zu Asche.
Doch Frankreichs schwere Wunden wird es heilen
Der Oelzweig in dem Mund der Taube sein,
Weissagend uns ein selig Friedensjahr. –
Du selber wirst alsbald ein andrer Mann
Denn siehe, eh' dies Oel dein Haupt dir netzt …

Heiliger, nie zu brechender Schwur in der
Neujahrsnacht 1873! –
Ich schwöre und gelobe auf das Feierlichste,
bei dem heiligen, reinen Zeichen der
Königlichen Lilien …

Opposite page: Secret Notes with triple Seal

The Private Diary of the King

These rare documents are original notes from Ludwig's diary. The notes are predominantly in French and are often signed 'Louis' *(opposite page)*. The translation of this triple-sealed entry reads, "The martyrdom of the holy Louis XVI give me the strength and power to overcome evil. May God help me." Again and again Ludwig would draw the lily of the Bourbons *(above)*, the symbol of virginal purity and God-given power. On occasions he would sign his entries in Spanish with *"Yo El Rey" (above centre)*. Parts of his diary are illegible, fragmentary, other parts bear witness to his passionate love of nature. The romantic atmosphere of his sleigh journeys is recorded. "In the magic of moonlight glid-ing through dark, snow-decked pines…" But such entries are insignificant compared to those dealing with his mental conflicts resulting from deep depression and a vain yearning for absolute purity. Disconnected sentences, mystic word fragments strive for expression. Such notes have been seen by many as proof of his madness – but they forget Ludwig's natural tendency to describe his emotions in effusive, sometimes pathetic terms. It was also an old tradition of the ruling Wittelsbachs to plumb the depths of their conscience in order to equip themselves for the coming day. In his insatiable desire for truth, Ludwig entrusted his last and most intimate secrets to his diary. In the year of his death he began a second diary, but of both diaries only the contents of a few pages are known. His entries are certainly not restricted to self-tormenting confessions. His dark and ever bolder plans to procure money, by whatever means, to continue his buildings were committed to his diaries – as was his bitter disappointment at failing to realise his plans.

du martyr du saint Roy Louis
me fortifie dans mes XVI
resolutions
et me donne la puissance à vaincre
le mal. —

Louis

donné à Hohenschwangau
le 21. janvier 1881.

Que Dieu vienne à mon aide

The Last Days of Youth pass by – Josef Kainz

"The *Separatvorstellung* is in full swing – suddenly, at a signal from the King, the rain machine is switched on. Masses of water pour down on decoration and costumes but the actors have to continue... until approving applause is heard from the King's box." This fictitious description is from the pen of Mark Twain, the American humorist, and was published in all seriousness by the world's press. In truth, the *Separatvorstellungen* were a great experience for the participating actors. Their sole spectator would never fail to offer some reward and the 23 year-old Kainz received a gift at his first performance.

"Farewell, they can do no more than hang me." With these words the young Josef Kainz took leave of his mother in Munich on 3rd July 1881 to travel to Linderhof as the King's guest. After a *Separatvorstellung* he had dispatched this invita-

tion and a sapphire ring to Kainz. However the King was disappointed by him in Linderhof and was near to sending him home. Hofrat Bürkel advised Kainz to act with more pathos – and the situation was saved. At the end of July Ludwig took him to Switzerland to the Vierwaldstättersee. The King travelled incognito but was everywhere recognized and enthusiastically greeted. Finally secluded accommodation was procured in the Villa Gutenberg near Mythenstein. Every evening a visit was made to the Rütli mountain, where Kainz recited Schiller's verse from Tell. On one occasion they did not arrive at the desired location until 2 a.m. but Kainz was still commanded to recite the Melchtal scene. He could not and collapsed with fatigue. Deeply hurt the King returned alone.

They met again in Lucerne. Ludwig accepted Kainz's apology saying "The matter is of no import". He then allowed himself to be photographed with Kainz. The illustrations show the King seated, Kainz standing *(left)* – they make a wretched, alarming impression. Could this be the King? Hopes disappointed, the blank gaze of a man tormented by frustrated desires he wishes to dissimilate. The young man next to him is the very person whom he covered with his own cape on the steamer trip to the Rütli, whom he lovingly woke from sleep to casually declare "You snore loudly". On this photograph we are presented with a haggard Josef Kainz listlessly awaiting the end of the journey so that he could sleep at length. The King no longer wished to see him but was impressed, when, having called off a *Separatvorstellung* in which Kainz was to appear, Kainz made him a gift of a painting of the Vierwaldstättersee. However, a genuine reconciliation never took place.

Opposite page:
Equestrian statue of King Louis XIV of France at Herrenchiemsee. Ludwig II saw the Sun King as the very personification of the word 'monarchy'. The architecture of French absolutism could be discerned in Linderhof, but this is more than surpassed by Herrenchiemsee, where the west front and Galerie des Glaces are even greater than at Versailles.

For the journey to Switzerland Ludwig ordered the police authorities to issue passports for himself and Kainz in the names of 'Marquis de Saverny' and 'Didier' – two characters from Victor Hugo's drama 'Marion de Lorme'. Kainz had played 'Didier' in a Separatvorstellung.

Opposite page above: View of the garden at Herrenchiemsee with the west façade.

Opposite page below: The hall of mirrors; 33 glass chandeliers with 1188 candles, 44 candelabras with 660 candles – all were lit for the King who would pace to and fro below them in his splendid isolation. Today the candles are lit for summer evening concerts.

The 'magic table' (below) was designed by the French Court mechanic Loriot for Louis XV's extravagant banquets at which the presence of servants was not desired. Ludwig II had this Tischlein-deck-dich copied so he could be alone with his dreams, undistracted by servants.

Schloss Herrenchiemsee

Interior decoration began in 1881 before completion of the outer structure. Hofbaudirector Georg Dollmann was responsible for planning but was succeeded by the versatile architect J. Hofmann, creator of the extravagant decoration. Herrenchiemsee is a unique tribute to the French Sun King, Louis XIV. It was a second Versailles, and with the murals, the stucco work, the furnishings and all the ornamentation, the decorative arts and crafts began to flourish in Munich, whose fantasies (and errors) were to be carried on into the 20th century. On the door of the porcelain room there is a porcelain plaque *(above)* showing, in a miniature medaillon, the 'only' Ludwig portrait in the whole Palace. In the cellar stood the iron 'lift' for the 'Tischlein-deck-dich' apparatus *(right)*. Such a lift was used here and in Linderhof. Only once, from 7th to 16th September 1885, did Ludwig reside here. Herrenchiemsee also houses the King Ludwig II Museum, built in 1924/25 and extended in 1928–1931.

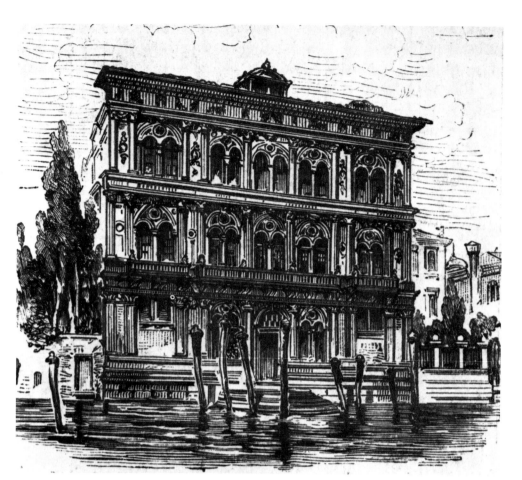

Richard Wagner's Death in the City of Lagoons

Left: The house where Richard Wagner died, the Palazzo Vendramin in Venice. On the day of his death an afternoon meal was to be taken as usual. The loyal gondolier Luigi brought soup. Wagner suddenly rose saying, "I feel very ill" and crashed unconscious to the floor. His doctor, Dr. Kepler, could only confirm his death.

Below: One of the last photographs of the composer.

On Shrove Tuesday 1883 Wagner rented a room near St. Mark's Square to witness the Venetian carneval. On Ash Wednesday he travelled to the island of San Michele by gondola. Before landing there he suffered a heart attack. His wife Cosima and a gondolier carried him into the small church in the cemetry where he regained consciousness. He died four days later.

"His body belongs to me" cried Ludwig when, in 1883, Hofrat Bürkel informed him of the death in Venice on 13th February of his adored musician friend. Ludwig's strength failed him and he sent an aide-de-camp to the burial. Venice reserved for the departed genius a magnificent funeral train. After the body had been returned to Wahnfried wreaths were sent in their hundreds – amongst them a last greeting from Ludwig. "To the composer of words and music, the maestro Richard Wagner, from Ludwig II of Bavaria", almost cold words betraying nothing of the exuberant emotions of past youth. Wagner's death heralded the impending fulfilment of Ludwig's proud prophecy in a letter to Wagner on 4th August 1865 – "When we two are no more, our work will serve the world as a shining example. It will delight generations, hearts will glow with enthusiasm for the artistic genius which is God-given and eternal".

Sorrow in Venice –
Tears in Bayreuth

Above: Funeral procession with Wagner's embalmed body, leading from the station in Bayreuth to Wahnfried, on 16th February 1883.
Right: "Last leave-taking", Cosima at Wagner's tomb, based on contemporary drawings.

Under the Yoke
of the Tyrant

"Nothing in the world would persuade me to be my own head of Cabinet" admitted Ludwig in a moment of openness – during his reign he made the lives of eight dutiful Cabinet heads miserable. After Pfistermeister, after Neumayr, Lutz and Lipowsky came August von Eisenhart *(below)*, a man whose fate it was to displease Ludwig at first sight. Nevertheless, he held his position for six years before he was summarily dismissed. "I cannot understand how I endured his stupid face for so long" was Ludwig's statement; in truth, Eisenhart had displayed qualities of zeal and great modesty. When, in 1871, His Majesty awarded him the *Komturkreuz des Kronenordens* he adjudged this too high an honour and humbly requested he be given a lesser distinction. Eisenhart's successor, Friedrich von Ziegler *(right)* brought more of an artistic nature to the King's Cabinet. At the outset he was accepted by the King "for lack of a better" but then won the right to address the King in the personal form. He wisely never made use of this right, although he received countless benevolent letters from the royal pen and once a long poem praising his virtues. An enormous burden of work was placed on each of Ludwig's heads of Cabinet, as Ziegler was also to learn. As the King never desired to see a

Minister, the *Kabinettschef* was Ludwigs's only spokesman. The Cabinet head also had to submit ministerial reports and applications to Ludwig for signature. Heavy physical demands were also placed on him. He had to stand when giving hours-long speeches and, on one occasion, the King forced him to stare at the dazzling surface of Lake Starnberg whilst speaking. Another time, he threatened him with a revolver, only to shake his head and utter, when Ziegler remained calm, "Look what kinds of things there are today, thermometers in the form of pistols." Since Ziegler had beautiful handwriting he was compelled to copy long reports. He also supervised Ludwig's activities, such as his reading, his building plans and his theatre visits. Often enough he was ordered to give lectures lasting through the night to the grey of the morning. In 1880 he was allowed to give up his rooms in the *Residenz* and to take a room in the city. When the King sent lackeys to fetch him in the middle of the night, they would only pretend to go and report that a dangerous dog had denied them entry to Ziegler's appartments. Strangely the King accepted this lie. Within three years Ziegler's strength was spent. After tendering his resignation on 6th September 1879 he was granted leave for medical reasons. In May 1880 the King forced him to return, but there were no more benevolent letters and their friendship was at an end. Relations became ever colder, they quarrelled and the formerly lively young man, who was all else but a bureaucrat, was finally drained of all strength a year later. The loyal servant took his leave. Others took his place... for a while; thereafter government business was conducted through lackeys.

1864

Time and Change

Silent but eloquent witnesses of an irreversible trend are the flourishes of Ludwig's ever-changing signature. The three examples shown here cover a period of two decades. No less of an impression is made by the portraits of the King which are also from the same period. The years have left their mark. The youthful figure of 1864 has made way for the broad-shouldered, corpulent figure of 1874, the sanguine eyes have taken on an imperious look, melancholy lines his face. This is how his Bavarian people saw him a year later in 1875 – and they celebrated him as on countless occasions before. In 1886 lonliness has marked him, his fate is almost upon him.

1874

The end draws near. Since early March 1886 moves were afoot in Munich to depose Ludwig. In May of that year the historian Otto Gerold met the King personally. He found him 'awkward', his face 'puffy', but added, "Nevertheless, his whole personality still bore the stamp of the unusual, he had the invincible quality of the ruler".

1886

"His Majesty is insane"

"His Majesty is, in advanced degree, insane and is suffering from that form of derangement known to alienists as paranoia". This is the first statement in a medical report, in which Ludwig II is declared incurably insane and unfit to rule for the rest of his life. On 8th June 1886 it was signed by Dr. von Gudden, the institute directors Dr. Hagen and Dr. Hubrich, and the university professor Dr. Grashey. With this report sentence was passed. None of the doctors had observed or examined Ludwig. The 'incriminating' evidence consisted of statements by lackeys and the King's notes which servants had been instructed to collect. Ludwig's last Cabinet Secretary Schneider had also made a collection of some 300 messages which Ludwig had sent to the Cabinet over the final three years – none of these betrayed any sign of derangement. Schneider waited to be questionned – but was never called. Hardly had Dr. von Gudden completed his report than a State Commission was formed. The commission dined with Luitpold the next day, 9th June, and then boarded a special train to Oberstdorf. There, Graf Holnstein, who had already deserted Ludwig, had made ready three fast coaches – the party reached Hohenschwangau at midnight.

Obermedizinalrat Dr. von Gudden, mental institute director and Professor of Psychiatry in Munich.

Freiherr Freyschlag von Freyenstein, aide-de-camp and advisor to Prince Luitpold. Through him Minister-President Lutz gained audience to Luitpold, Ludwig's uncle. The issue for discussion was the deposition of Ludwig and Lutz was one of the main actors. But what grounds did he and the Ministry have?

Minister-President Freiherr von Lutz, ennobled by his King, was the driving force behind the attempt to depose Ludwig.

Prince Otto's Fate awaits Ludwig

The two photographs on this page showing the deranged Prince Otto between two warders are staggering documents. In the photograph *(above left)* is Dr. Franz Carl Müller who accompanied Gudden to Hohenschwangau. Prince Otto was confined, for more than ten years, in total isolation at Schloss Fürstenried. He was no longer troubled by excitable states which, in the past, only his brother Ludwig had been able to calm. He lived out his dull-witted life, a helpless wreck. High state officials, two doctors and four brutal warders were soon to subject King Ludwig to a far worse fate.

Dramatic Hours in Schwangau

Below Neuschwanstein *(below: view from the balcony of the throne room)* in the feeble light of an ominous sky, the land lay peaceful on the evening of 10th June 1886. The commission had taken up quarters in the old Schloss Hohenschwangau. The leader was the State Minister Freiherr Krafft von Crailsheim *(right)*. He was accompanied by Reichsrat Graf von Törring-Jettenbach, Legationsrat Dr. Rumpler and the tall Freiherr von Washington, confident of Prince Luitpold and selected as the future "companion" of the King. Graf Holnstein was also of the party – a serious error of judgement, but they were relying for support on his robust nature. The main personnage, however, was Dr. von Gudden who had brought along his assistant Dr. Müller and four sturdy warders. The seven-course meal which was set before these officials was entitled 'Souper de sa Majesté le Roi'. They fortified themselves royally, drinking forty quarts of beer and ten bottles of champagne with the meal.

Dr. von Gudden discussed plans for the coming dawn. Everything seemed easy. The King would be approached – but by whom? "By me" spoke up Graf Holnstein, "It does not trouble me, I will not hesitate." His voice had an unpleasant edge. Hearing the sound of horses in the courtyard, he dashed outside. Ludwig's coachman, Osterholzer, was pre-

A nervous State Minister: Freiherr Krafft von Crailsheim. He carried a declaration from Ludwig's uncle, Prince Luitpold, but had no opportunity to deliver it.

paring for the King's nightly drive. Holnstein cried, "Unharness the horses. The King gives no more orders." The arrival of the party had seemed strange to the loyal Osterholzer, but now he knew enough. Had not the castle guard Schramm said that the company included four asylum warders? Beside himself with fear he hastened up the path through the forest to Neuschwanstein. The King was preparing for his ride. Osterholzer threw himself at Ludwig's feet, babbled out his story and implored his King to flee. Weber, the valet, expressed his willingness to join them but Ludwig refused. Why shoud he flee? If there were any danger, Hesselschwerdt whom he had sent to Munich would have warned him. Head groom Hesselschwerdt, his long-time confident via whom he communicated with his Ministries, had betrayed him and along with the valet Mayr

A dubious gentleman: Graf Holnstein. Although earlier a close friend of Ludwig's, he was an active member of the commission.

A fearless lady: Baronin Truchsess with her parasol which she brandished like a sword to gain entrance to the castle.

had turned witness against him. Ludwig did, however, give orders to defend the castle. When the party arrived at 4 a.m., they were confronted by police with loaded rifles. It was cold and rainy. The fire brigades from surrounding villages appeared out of the drifting fog. Police and chasseurs had alarmed the whole of Schwangau and peasants flocked in to protect their King. In vain did the commissioners show their written authority. "We know only the King's command" cried the sergeant Heinze as the commission approached the castle gate, "Not one step further or we fire". The party was forced back, a rifle butt struck one of the warders. A bottle broke and the sweet smell of chloroform filled the cold morning air. At the same time a shrill female voice was heard. Baronin Truchsess, recently released from a mental institute, had come to protect her King. She had

arrived unnoticed and now she intervened loudly, brandishing her parasol. An eye witness reported: "The Baronin knew the members of the commission personally from Munich and heaped violent abuse on them on account of their treacherous behaviour. 'Minister von Crailsheim' she cried, 'Never again will I play piano with you. Graf Törring, your children should be ashamed of you.' She invited all to join in a cry of 'Long live the King' and, waving her parasol wildly, forced her way into the castle. 'Did that wretched woman have to come just now!' cursed Holnstein..." Angry glances and threatening shouts greeted him. The commission, admitting inglorious defeat, withdrew. Back in Munich, the fiasco was officially declared to have been "insignificant" – but the story quickly spread through the whole of Bavaria.

"Arrest them" instructed Ludwig upon learning the names of the members of the commission. Each name, in particular that of Graf Holnstein, called forth a fresh outburst of rage, and maddened with anger he dispatched servants with ever new commands. The prisoners were to be brought to the castle – thrown into cells – flogged – have an eye put out – skinned alive... The King wished to punish this breach of loyalty with medieval cruelty. Rage drove him from room to

room – gone are the hours in which genius favoured him. Hardly had the commissioners returned to Hohenschwangau than Captain Sonntag from Füssen appeared to arrest them. *Chevauxlegers* were already on the way to intercept them with yet new orders from the King. The prisoners were to be chained. This they were spared as the police had no chains. Their journey was not without danger, as was revealed in Dr. Müller's record, he being arrested along with Dr. von Gudden and Baron Washington. "As we passed the Alpenrose inn in Hohenschwangau, there stood a group of about twenty, looking as though they could happily tear us to pieces. In the castle courtyard we had to run the gauntlet through a large mob of similar figures, firemen, peasants and lumbermen". The prisoners were locked in the first floor of the gate house *(opposite page)*. From its windows the dark walls of the castle courtyard *(right)* could be seen. Holnstein, in shirt-sleeves, threw himself on the bed. To command respect he had shouted in the courtyard, "I desire breakfast immediately". He was ignored. The situation was unpleasant. Holnstein and Törring-Jettenbach scratched their names on the walls, as do condemned men. The names are still visible today *(below)*. After three hours imprisonment, however, they were released one by one at intervals – for which the valet Mayr was probably to be thanked. As the state officials were fleeing in a trap from Hohenschwangau Graf Dürckheim, aide-de-camp to the King, passed in the opposite direction without greeting them. The doctors and warders had to make their own way back. An eye witness reported: "Dr. von Gudden was most afraid for his life. He requested Captain Sonntag to take him to Füssen in his coach as he feared the angry population would mistreat him. Sonntag consoled him with a cigar and calmed him...". The luckless commission regained Munich late in the evening.

Minister-President Lutz conferred with Prince Luitpold behind closed doors until 1 o'clock in the morning.

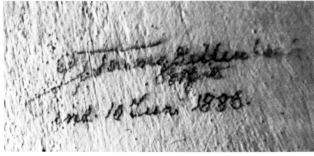

Following Pages 130/131:

Left: The Throne Room in Neuschwanstein, the only room in the Byzantine style.

Right: Neuschwanstein: in the style of the German medieval castles, built from 1869–1886. Some parts, such as the square tower, remained uncompleted during Ludwig's lifetime.

The King's Loyal Paladin

Graf Dürckheim (*opposite page*) was aide-de-camp to Prince Arnulf – until 1880 when he challenged him to a duel because of the Prince's excessive interest in his wife. Ludwig forbade the duel, appointed Dürckheim captain and, at the same time, his adjutant general. With the arrival of this resolute young officer at Neuschwanstein he now had royal support but he no longer had the will to act. Dürckheim requested Ludwig to accompany him to Munich at once for "any intrigue will collapse as soon as the people see the King". Baronin Truchsess who was still present provided enthusiastic agreement and expressed the wish to join them. It was only with difficulty that the eccentric lady was persuaded to leave. Then several telegrams were dispatched, one to Bismarck who immediately advised Ludwig to defend his own interests personally in Munich. For the Chancellor this would have been proof of Ludwig's ability to rule. Two telegrams from the War Ministry ordered Dürckheim's return to Munich. Ludwig allowed him to go – thus recognizing the authority of the new government. His last paladin was arrested at Munich station on a charge of high treason.

That night the King wandered restlessly through the lonely castle. The police at the castle gate had been replaced by men of the new government, the telephone (*far right*) could not be used, no heat came from the heating vent (*right*), a great innovation of the time. Almost all the servants had made off.

Above: The Minstrels' Hall, inspired by the Festsaal at Wartburg, was part of the earliest plans for Neuschwanstein.

In the bedroom Tristan and Isolde look down from the walls reminding the King of his boundless joy on 10th June 1865, the première of Wagner's 'Tristan and Isolde' in Munich. In the front centre of the illustration is Ludwig's wash-stand. Running water issued from the silver swan.

Opposite page, above: View of the waterfall in the Pöllat gorge seen from the King's bed.

Opposite page, below: Therese Lang, wife of the servant Vicentius Lang. She was the King's chambermaid at Neuschwanstein. On this final night the bed remained untouched.

The loyal servant Weber, a 24 year-old *chevauxleger*, had remained. Suddenly he was asked by the King, "Do you believe in the immortality of the soul?" – "Yes, your Majesty" – "So do I", said the King. "I have read many books, according to which one can become insane but what they are doing to me shall not go unpunished". Unable to contain himself, he cried, "That they take my throne, that I can endure, but that they declare me insane, that I cannot survive". Weber described this conversation and his honesty was not to be doubted when he reported that the King had given him his last money, 1200 marks, and a diamond clasp he used to wear on one of his hats. He also wrote a note guaranteeing Weber 25000 marks for the clasp should the Treasury demand its return.

Hastily Ludwig drank large amounts of white wine and cognac. Earlier he had demanded poison, to no avail. Now he said to Weber they should search for his head in the Pöllat gorge when Hoppe, the barber, came the next day. Thereafter he called Mayr, his valet, and demanded the key to the tower. Mayr, who was awaiting Dr. Gudden's return, replied that the key had been misplaced but he would search for it immediately – thus he escaped Ludwig's penetrating stare. For one whole year Mayr had been constrained to appear before Ludwig wearing a black mask as the King had no desire to see his face. Mayr was the most enthusiastic collector of information to incriminate the King and, along with Hesselschwerdt, made the most damning testimony. The servant Buchner, a simple type, had to bear a wax seal on his forehead to indicate that his mind was sealed. Another lackey had to wear jester's clothing and was seated on a donkey. All servants had to scratch on doors to beg entry and to approach their ruler on their knees.

The 'gang' of Ministers was to be thrown in a dungeon (there were no dungeons at any of the castles). The Prussian Crown Prince was to be chained in a cave to languish and whimper on bread and water. To raise money for his building projects Ludwig gave the command to rob banks. It is no coincidence that he wished to build his new castle 'Falkenburg' on a rocky cliff in the style of a 'robber knights' castle'. Ludwig's final tragedy had begun because of his precarious finances. He had been fervently attempting to obtain money but had been refused everywhere. On 6th April 1886 Bismarck had given him good advice. Since no state money but only the King's income had been squandered, he should appeal to the Bavarian *Landtag* to put his Treasury in order. Ludwig issued immediate orders to his Ministry – but these were countermanded. "If I cannot build, I cannot live" he would often say. Now, for a second time, a medical commission was on its way.

Witness of Stone

On the morning of 12th June at half past midnight, Dr. von Gudden arrived at Neuschwanstein with Dr. Müller, a head warder and four assistant warders. The valet Mayr explained hastily that his Majesty *(above)* was in a state of great excitation and had repeatedly demanded the key to the tower. Gudden and his group hurried to a corridor which ended by the door to the tower near the King's rooms. Warders and police were posted in the staircase where a stone dragon rears up to guard access to the tower *(opposite page)*.

Mayr handed the key to the King. Dr. Müller was later to report: "Suddenly we heard firm footsteps and a man of imposing stature stood at the door to the corridor... the warders approached, cut off his retreat and seized him by the arms...".

The 'Lost' Key to the Tower

Instead of climbing the narrow spiral staircase of the tower *(opposite page)*, the King could have thrown himself out of the window to his death. Some believe he had hidden his secret diary in a niche in the tower wall and wished to guard it from prying eyes. Dr. Müller's report depicts how the dark events continued after the warders had seized Ludwig. "The King let out a surprised 'Ah' and then repeated again and again 'What do you want? Release me' He was led to his bedroom where the warders secured the windows and doors to prevent him jumping to his death. Gudden (acting on behalf of Prince Luitpold) then said: 'Your Majesty, it is the saddest action of my life that I perform now. Four alienists have provided a report on your Majesty and in the light of their findings Prince Luitpold has taken over the government. I have my orders to accompany your Majesty to Schloss Berg this very night'. The King, it was noted, could hardly control himself and finally said, 'How can you declare me insane? You have not yet examined me' – 'Your Majesty, it was not necessary, the overwhelming documentary evidence is proof enough'.

There followed an agonizing three and a half hour wait because the coaches had not arrived in time. One of the warders, Bruno Mauder, also left notes. He mentioned Gudden had informed the King that the alienists had sworn an oath to the accuracy of the medical report. Mauder's simple report then goes on, "His Majesty said to Gudden there was much perjury at the moment, it was a conspiracy, he knew it. Luitpold had made his arrangements very well, a charming comedy, Luitpold was a sly one. In all seriousness his Majesty pointed out that Gudden was a Prussian, whereupon Gudden retorted that he was a Bavarian citizen and all his children had been born in Bavaria". Dr. von Gudden originated from Cleve, Rhenish Prussia, and was a naturalized Bavarian.

Bekanntmachung, die Uebernahme der Regentschaft und die Einberufung des Landtages betr.

Im Namen Seiner Majestät des Königs.

Unser Königliches Haus und Bayerns treubewährtes Volk ist nach Gottes unerforschlichem Rathschlusse von dem erschütternden Ereignisse betroffen worden, daß Unser vielgeliebter Neffe, der allerdurchlauchtigste großmächtigste König und Herr, **Seine Majestät König Ludwig II.,** an einem schweren Leiden erkrankt sind, welches Allerhöchstdieselben an der Ausübung der Regierung auf längere Zeit im Sinne des Titels II § 11 der Verfassungs-Urkunde hindert.

Da Seine Majestät der König für diesen Fall Allerhöchst Selbst weder Vorsehung getroffen haben, noch dermalen treffen können, und da ferner über Unseren vielgeliebten Neffen, **Seine Königliche Hoheit den Prinzen Otto von Bayern,** ein schon länger andauerndes Leiden verhängt ist, welches Ihm die Uebernahme der Regentschaft unmöglich macht, so legen Uns die Bestimmungen der Verfassungsurkunde als nächstberufenem Agnaten die traurige Pflicht auf, die Reichsverwesung zu übernehmen.

Indem Wir Dieses, von dem tiefsten Schmerze ergriffen, öffentlich kund und zu wissen thun, verfügen Wir hiemit in Gemäßheit des Titels II §§ 11 und 16 der Verfassungs-Urkunde die Einberufung des Landtages auf **Dienstag den 15. Juni lfd. Js.**

Die k. Kreisregierungen werden beauftragt, **sofort** alle aus ihrem Kreise berufenen Abgeordneten für die zweite Kammer unter abschriftlicher Mittheilung dieser öffentlichen Ausschreibung aufzufordern, sich rechtzeitig in der Haupt- und Residenzstadt München einzufinden.

München, den 10. Juni 1886.

Luitpold
Prinz von Bayern.

Dr. Frhr. v. Lutz. Dr. v. Fäustle. Dr. v. Riedel. Frhr. v. Crailsheim. Frhr. v. Feilitzsch. v. Heinleth.

Auf höchsten Befehl:
Der Ministerialrath im k. Staatsministerium des Innern,
v. Neumayr.

Left: The Regency declaration of Prince Luitpold on 10th June 1886.

Below: A special edition of the 'Münchner Fremdenblatt' of 11th June 1886. The sentence, "The commission was clapped in chains in Hohenschwangau" was incorrect. The official announcement "...that his Majesty is in Hohenschwangau and is receiving the most considerate medical treatment" is also not a true reflection of the facts. Contradictory and absurd rumours, often of a malicious nature, were put about.

Die letzten zuverlässigen Nachrichten

aus

Hohenschwangau

lauten:

Die Staatskommission, welche Sr. Majestät dem Könige die Nachricht von der Regentschaftübernahme durch Se. kgl. Hoheit Prinz Luitpold überbringen sollte, ist gestern Abend unverrichteter Sache wieder hieher zurückgekehrt. Die ganze Kommission war gefesselt in Hohenschwangau internirt und war die Aufregung der dortigen Bevölkerung, welche Sr. Maj. dem Könige zu Hilfe eilen wollte, eine derartige, daß für das Leben der einzelnen Mitglieder der Kommission große Befürchtungen eintraten.

Das Bezirksamt Füssen verhalf letzterer zur Flucht, dieselbe war aber gezwungen, um rasch von der Stelle zu kommen, das Gepäck zurückzulassen, welches erst heute Mittag hier eintrifft. — Bei der Ankunft der Kommission in Hohenschwangau rief S. M. der König den Grafen von Dürckheim zu Hilfe und Letzterer, von dem Stande der Dinge nicht unterrichtet, trat als Opponent auf.

Heute ist abermals eine Anzahl Gendarmerie nach Hohenschwangau abgegangen. Herr Gendarmerie-Oberst von Hellingrath traf gestern mit seinem Adjutanten an Ort und Stelle die nöthigen Dispositionen zur Entsetzung der Staatskommission. Das neue Schloß in Hohenschwangau ist nun vollständig isolirt, allein die Pflege Sr. Maj. des Königs hatte bis gestern Abend noch nicht beginnen können, da Se. Maj. der König Jedermann den Zutritt untersagt.

Amtlich wird gemeldet, daß sich Se. Majestät in Hohenschwangau befinden und daß die ärztliche Behandlung Derselben in schonendster Weise bereits begonnen hat.

Prelude to
the Last Act

In vain had the peasants and the mountain folk assembled to help the King flee. In vain had the Tirolean chasseurs prepared to defend him across the Austrian border. Now three coaches were making their way through rain and mist via Weilheim and Seeshaupt to Berg. Leading were Dr. Müller, the valet Mayr and two warders. In the middle coach, which could not be opened from the inside, sat Ludwig, alone. Barth, the head warder, was outside on the coach box. Gudden with Captain Horn and two warders brought up the rear. With head lowered, Fritz Schwegler, once an outrider seen only at the head of the King's horses, followed on behind. In Seeshaupt the horses were changed for the third time and greys were harnessed.

Upon Ludwig's request, Frau Anna Vogl, the post mistress, tearfully brought him a glass of water and was profusely thanked. They exchanged a few words and as the coaches pulled away, Frau Vogl dispatched a messenger on horseback to Empress Elisabeth in Possenhofen.

At midday the carriages reached Schloss Berg. There the alienist Dr. Grashey, Gudden's son-in-law, had been at work. Door handles had been removed, spy-holes drilled in the doors and holes made in the window-frames to accommodate iron bars. Ludwig complained to the warder Mauder who served him a modest meal. The King then retired to bed and Mauder reports: "It was a quarter to three in the afternoon. I received his Majesty's command to wake him in nine hours. He fell asleep after a few minutes. I informed Dr. Müller of my command to wake the King. He replied that his Majesty would not be wakened and should be brought to lead a life where day was day and night was night."

The post office at Seeshaupt with a picture of Ludwig II.

Whit Sunday,
13th June 1886

Ludwig woke shortly before 1 o'clock. Warders Braun and Schneller were on night duty. They refused to give him his clothes. He wandered for some hours in his nightshirt and stockings. At six in the morning Mauder returned and noted that: "His Majesty needed twelve pails of water to wash". After breakfast Ludwig took a walk with Gudden, two warders followed and police were posted in the park. Gudden returned in good humour and declared that the King (*opposite page: last photograph*) was just a child. Twenty two years previously Ludwig had chosen Schloß Berg (*left*) as his summer residence (*below*) and now he was confined here by force. But this troubled no-one. Gudden was satisfied and dispatched an optimistic telegram to Lutz in Munich. "Everything is going splendidly here".

Gudden: "We will go alone"

The King dined at 4 in the afternoon, alone and not without annoyance that an attempt had been made to mix drugs into his food, so as to present him to his people as deserving of the treatment he was receiving. He had been refused permission to attend early-morning mass in Aufkirchen, to avoid unnecessary attention. After his meal he received his former head chef Zander, who had been obliged by Gudden to refuse to discuss with Ludwig any plans for escape. Zander reported: "The King came up to me, his eyes blazing with energy and life as in his best days and very different from 48 hours before. In both rooms he showed me the window bolts, the holes in the doors, everything that indicated they considered him raving mad". Ludwig then asked him whether he would be kept prisoner for long. When Zander attempted to console him with talk of an early recovery and release, the King interposed: "Do you really believe that? My uncle Luitpold will grow so accustomed to ruling and take such pleasure from it that he will never release me". Ludwig then asked if the police in the park were carrying loaded rifles and if they would shoot at him. Zander answered that the rifles were not loaded and it would be unthinkable to shoot at his Majesty. Ludwig then ushered him into a corner by the window, out of view of the spy-hole.

Zander had the impression the King wished to impart something of importance, remembered his promise to Gudden and requested the King to discharge him. Ludwig began to speak again, Zander took fear and repeated his request... "and then, that dark expression suddenly clouded the King's face, the expression he always had when his mistrust was aroused. He said nothing more and signalled me to leave". Shortly after 6 o'clock Ludwig and Gudden set out on their second walk as agreed. The warder Mauder remembered the following: "The King went ahead, Gudden a few steps behind. In front of the castle Gudden turned and said 'We will go alone'". Mauder passed on these orders to Dr. Müller and to the two warders in the castle who were making ready to follow. The water-colour by H. Breling (opposite page) does not quite portray the truth. Dr. von Gudden gave his orders directly before the castle. Under a threatening sky they set off – the giant figure of the King in his black overcoat and broadrimmed hat, the doctor in a top hat. On the previous evening flickering torches had been seen, boats had been moored at the lakeside. The King is also said to have received a signal from the undergrowth during his morning walk – but there were no witnesses to the events that followed and the mystery remains.

The King is dead...

Where the body was found on the east bank of Lake Starnberg. Ludwig's watch showed 6.54, water had penetrated between the face and the glass. Gudden's had stopped at 8 o'clock.

When Gudden had not returned by 8 o'clock, Dr. Müller became alarmed and sent policemen into the park. According to his notes two policemen constantly patrolled the park but they later reported having seen and heard nothing. Then Baron Washington, the castle administrator Huber and almost all the castle staff searched the park. Müller and Huber directed their attention to a rocky section. All was to no avail. Shortly before ten o'clock a telegram was sent to Munich. "The King and Gudden have taken a evening stroll, not yet returned, the park is being searched". The agitation was indescribable. At 10.30 Ludwig's hat with the diamond clasp, his overcoat and jacket were found by the bank, then Gudden's hat and umbrella. Dr. Müller reported: "I ran with Huber down to the lake. We woke a fisherman, clambered into a boat and at 11 o'clock rowed towards Leoni. We had not been on the water long when Huber suddenly uttered a cry and jumped into the water, which came up to his chest. He caught hold of a body floating in the water – it was the King's, a few yards away was Gudden's body. I pulled him into the boat and the fisherman made for the shore".

Ludwig's body being taken from the lake. At 6'3" he was exceptionally tall.

Ludwig lying in State in Schloss Berg

Dr. Müller's medical findings: "The King bore no injuries to his body (but the rim of his hat was torn). Gudden's face showed several oblique scratches on forehead and nose. Above his right eye was a not insignificant bruise, certainly caused by a blow of the fist. The nail of Gudden's right-hand middle finger was half ripped off". After Empress Elisabeth had left Ludwig's death bed on Whit Monday, the country people who had been waiting impatiently were allowed into the castle. In the greatest of agitation peasants, fishermen, women and children saw that their King was dead. Many dropped to their knees, others cursed Dr. von Gudden and threatened the servants, others still ripped pieces from the linen on which Ludwig lay and kissed them. "Our Father,..." screeched a shrill female voice, a prayer which all present took up.

Extra-Blatt

Volkswirthſchaftliche,

Neueſte Nachrichten
und
Münchener Anzeiger.

Alpine & Sport-Zeitung

München, Montag 14. Juni.

39. Jahrgang. 1886.

Früh 7 Uhr.

Nachdem Seine Majeſtät der König ſeit der Ankunft in Schloß Berg den ärztlichen Rathſchlägen ruhige Folge geleiſtet hatten, machten Allerhöchſtdieſelben geſtern Abends 6¾ Uhr in Begleitung des Obermedizinalrathes Dr. von Gudden einen Spaziergang in den Park, von dem Allerhöchſtdieſelben und Dr. von Gudden längere Zeit nicht zurückgekehrt ſind. Nach Durch-ſuchung des Parkes und des Seeufers wurden Seine Majeſtät mit dem Obermedizinalrath Dr. von Gudden im See gefunden. — Seine Majeſtät gaben gleichwie Dr. von Gudden anfangs noch ſchwache Lebenszeichen. Die von Dr. Müller vorgenommenen Wiederbelebungs-verſuche waren jedoch vergeblich. Um 12 Uhr Nachts wurde der Tod Seiner Majeſtät kon-ſtatirt. Gleiches war bei Dr. von Gudden der Fall.

München, den 14. Juni 1886.

Königliche Polizeidirektion.

The News of Ludwig's Death
causes a Great Stir

Until his entombment special newspaper editions were pub-lished, sometimes up to four a day *(opposite page)*. There was nothing new to report but the public did not seem to tire of reading the same information over and over again. Mean-while Graf (later Fürst) Philipp zu Eulenburg, secretary of the Prussian legation in Munich, had written an extraordi-nary letter to his friend Fritz von Farenheid-Beynuhnen: "I have well endured the great excitement that has attended the royal drama. It was of remarkable interest to personally witness this most unbelievable of recent catastrophes. Privy to the plans of the State to depose the unfortunate King, I was also involved in the events at Hohenschwangau where the King, in his madness, condemned to death the commis-sion which had come to announce his deposition. I was also woken in that night at Starnberg when the King and Dr. von Gudden were found in the water near Berg. I will never forget that impression as I rowed across the lonely lake with the fisherman Jakob Ernst in the early morning mist. The silence of death shrouded Schloss Berg; pale and numb stood the servants in the courtyard and in the corridors as I hurried, with a beating heart, to the room where the legend-ary King had just been laid to rest, an insane smile on his ashen lips, his black curls defiant upon his white forehead. My dismayed questions remained unanswered. I had to piece together for myself what had transpired. In the next room lay Dr. von Gudden, dead, a sombre look upon his face. I saw the scar upon his forehead, the frightful marks of strangulation on his thick neck. He had been strangled by

the King when attempting to prevent his suicide. I was the first to examine the scene of the struggle by daylight. I saw the King's footprints deep below the surface. They could not have been made by someone attempting to flee towards the centre of the lake. The King who was a strong swimmer could have escaped to the left or right to the shore and left no marks on the lake bed. He had purposefully driven him-self to his own death. From the point where the unmistak-able signs of the struggle with Dr. Gudden could be seen, the steps of the King traced a line away from the shore to-wards his death."

These last sentences by Eulenburg are contradicted by other observers who also examined the traces left in the clay bed of the lake and drew different conclusions. It is of interest that the secretary of the Prussian legation had personally witnessed all previous events but had remained discreetly in the background. The fact that he was in Starnberg at Whit-sun was also no coincidence. It was strange that Dr. Müller never mentioned 'the frightful marks of strangulation' on Gudden's neck. Later he did testify that 'for reasons un-known' a post-mortem was not performed on the body. The cause of Gudden's death remained a mystery. A post-mor-tem was carried out on the King's body by Obermedizinalrat Kerschensteiner and anatomy professor Rüdiger. Their re-port contained nothing more than 'a confirmation of the re-port on Ludwig's mental health'. These 'findings' were sub-jected to great criticism – but the cause of death was never revealed.

☛ **Preis 10 Pfennig.**

Viertes Extrablatt

des

 „Gemeindebürger". ☞

Ausgegeben 15. Juni um 2½ Uhr Nachmittags.

Originalbericht.

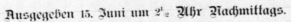 **Warum man den König nach Berg gebracht.**

In Hohenschwangau und Umgegend war die Erregung groß. Der König selbst wurde erst durch Oberregierungsrath von Müller beruhigt.

Ehe er Hohenschwangau verließ, that er die Aeußerung:

„Daß man mir die Regierung nimmt, das ertrag ich, aber daß man mich für irrsinnig erklärt, das überleb ich nicht."

Solche Aeußerungen steigerten die Erregung und man fürchtete sich, den König nach dem Linderhof zu bringen, um der Tyroler willen.

Zweimal war alles zur Flucht des Königs vorbereitet. Aber er verschmähte es, zu fliehen.

„Wollte ich der Sache entgehen, so stürzte ich mich in die Schlucht herab vom Thurm."

Als der König aus dem Zimmer trat, griffen ihm zwei Wärter unter die Arme. Er warf Dr. von Gudden einen langen finsteren Blick zu. Dann stieg er allein in den Wagen, seinen Wagen, nicht den Irrenhauswagen, den man herangebracht. Dann ging die Fahrt, vorneauf saß ein Oberwärter, mit doppeltem Relaiwechsel nach Berg.

Hier kannte der König jede Gelegenheit für sein Vorhaben — er hat sie benützt. Die Stelle, wo der König auf der Flucht zum See durchgebrochen, liegt auf Mitte Weges vom Schloß zu Leoni. Gebüsch ist geknickt, zwei Fähnlein bezeichnen die Stelle, zwei kleine Hölzchen den Platz, wo Rock und Hut des Königs lagen. Gudden hat den König zu halten versucht, Mit einem Ruck hat der König beide Röcke, die Aermel ineinander, fahren lassen.

Dann gings hinein in den See. Es war ein wüthender Kampf. Dann folgte Ruhe — die Ruhe des Todes.

Der See that sein Werk und spülte die Leichen heran. Nur 10 Meter vom Ufer lagerten die Leichen friedlich bei einander — —

Die Leiche des Königs in München.

Der Sektion des Königs, die in dem sog. Marterzimmer, oberhalb der Hofkapelle in der Residenz vorgenommen wird, wohnen 8—10 Herren bei, darunter der langjährige Leibarzt des Königs

Dr. Schleiß,

der sich von seiner Krankheit nicht überzeugen will.

Auch Professor Ziemssen, die bekannte Autorität, ist zugegen.

Gleich nach der Sektion findet die Einbalsamirung statt, die Dr. Nobiling vornimmt.

Redaktion und Verlag von Josef Morgenstern, München. Druck von J. A. Beck, München, Zweigstr. 4.

Thousands pay their Last Respects

At about 9 o'clock in the evening Ludwig's body was taken to Munich. The sound of weeping escorted the procession, whole villages turned out to pay their last honours. The coffin passed Schloss Fürstenried, the castle in which the new King Otto, Ludwig's brother who was also unfit to rule, was confined to live out his dull-witted life. From Sendling the guard of honour was formed by a troop of *chevauxlegers*. On 15th June, at 3 a.m., Ludwig arrived in the *Residenz*. In the old chapel, where he had awarded many of his faithful the Order of St. George, Ludwig's mortal remains were laid in state – in the black velvet dress of the Grand Master of the Order of St. Hubertus. His head rested on a coat of ermin, around his neck hung the chain of the Order, studded with precious stones. His left hand rested on the handle of the ancient sword of the Order, his right pressed the jasmine blossoms of Empress Elisabeth to his breast. This sombre figure towered above the Knights of the Order of St. George, who kept the last watch in their red uniforms, and the bodyguards with their halberts. Lighted candles framed the coffin.

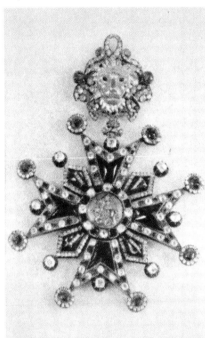

The Stillness of Death – and Secretive Whispers

Above the catafalque a crown supported a black canopy. The high altar was covered with a black cloth with a white cross from which shone the royal coat of arms. For three days men and women of all ages and rank took leave of their King in deep reverence. The dense masses were joined by ever new groups arriving from the Bavarian countryside. Weather-hardened hunters, fishermen, lumbermen, peasants and their wives in traditional festive costume kneeled and made the sign of the cross, eyes brimming with tears. Many simply stared, spell-bound, at the body of the King, rooted to the spot as the crowds pushed by them. They noticed nothing of the trappings of the occasion, they sought only to look upon that face already familiar to them from personal encounters. They stopped, nodded meaningfully, eyes wide and hearts beating furiously. They were convinced they had seen a face of wax, that a wax figure had been placed in the coffin and this was not the King. Informed persons later suggested that Ludwig's face had been covered with a film of wax to lend him dignity. In the mountains, however, the myth was born that the King and Gudden had been exiled and wax figures buried in their place. The fisherman Jakob Lidl who was present when Ludwig's and Gudden's bodies were taken from the lake was often asked: "Lidl, didn't you rescue wax figures from the lake?". He made no reply as long as he lived. But later we shall learn of a document that is said to have been written by him.

Above right: The Bavarian royal crown: headband with eight bands meeting to support a globe and cross.

Above center: Cross of the Order of St. Hubertus, a Maltese cross with precious stones.

Below: Order of the Knights of St. George.

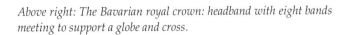

Das Bouquet der Kaiserin.

Das Bouquet, welches Kaiserin Elisabeth geschickt und das die Brust des Königs ziert, wird nach Carlsbad geschickt und dort versteinert werden. Bei der Umlegung des Sarges in den großen Zinnsarg wird das Bouquet wieder zur Leiche gelegt werden.

Die

Wahrheit

über das

Leben u. Sterben

König Ludwig II.

Eine kurze, wahrheitsgetreue Darstellung von Allem, was sich in den Tagen vom 10. bis 19. Juni 1886 in München, Hohenschwangau und Schloß Berg zugetragen hat.

Dem königstreuen bayerischen Volke
am Begräbnißtage König Ludwig II. gewidmet.

Preis 10 Pfg. — Zu haben: Zeitungs-Expedition Landschaftsstraße Nr. 11. — Preis 10 Pfg.

Newspaper report (above) concerning a vanished custom: the last bouquet from Kaiserin Elisabeth was 'carved in stone'.

Left: The first newspaper article claiming to write the 'truth' about the life and death of Ludwig II. It heralded a flood of similar publications.

Below: An example of an announcement by means of which art dealers offered portraits 'in remembrance of our beloved Ludwig II'.

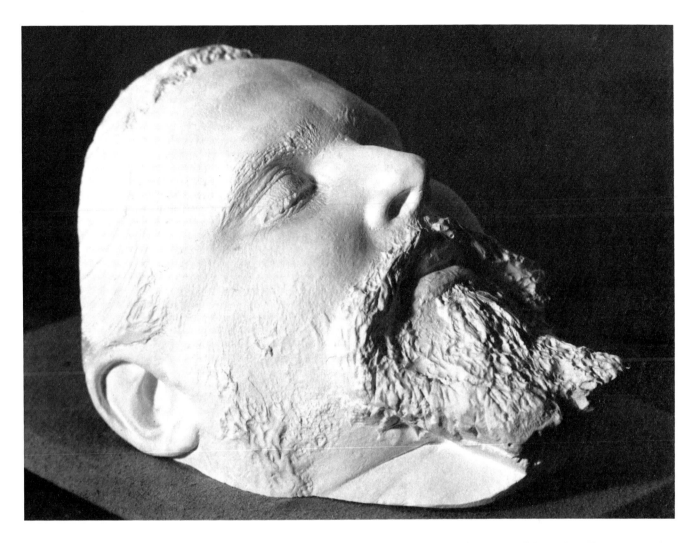

The Death Mask of Ludwig II

Gottfried von Böhm who saw the dead King wrote: "I did not find him to be disfigured or to wear a tyrannical, dominating expression as some who saw him before he was embalmed had maintained. The death mask which had already been made in Berg also does not have such an expression. On the contrary a slight, almost ironic smile plays upon his lips. His rigid features show no sign of madness. He was at peace". The same opinion was shared by the Prussian Crown Prince who addressed the following noble, heart-felt words to the King's mother on 18th June 1886: "Today I saw the face of your dear son for the last time, fifteen years having elapsed since I had seen him previously. Peace and tranquillity rested upon his features, the beauty of which death could not take from him. People of all rank crowded in great masses to see him".

Right: A lock of the King's hair exhibited, as is the death mask, in Ludwig II Museum, Herrenchiemsee.

151

*"In the name of His Majesty King Otto,
His Royal Highness Prince Luitpold
is hereby declared Prince-Regent of Bavaria"*

Special edition of the 'Neueste Nachrichten' of 14th June 1886. The Constitution states: "The crown is hereditary in the male line of the royal family according to the law of the first born and to the rights of agnatic linear succession. Suc-

Farewell for ever

Newspaper report of 17th June: "The crush of mourning folk to the old chapel in the Residenz *(above)* was without end. A lady who had fainted was almost trampled to death. Yesterday a total of 20 people fainted and a mountain of lost tresses, bustles and broken umbrellas bore testimony to the rigours to which the people subjected themselves. Pickpockets were also hard at work". – The funeral procession *(right)* on 18th June was headed by the clergy. As a symbol of death the hearse was preceded by the 'Gugelmänner'. They carried lighted candles crossed at the breast and a 'Gugel', a cowled hood which hid their faces. The newspapers published poems, the 'Bayerisches Vaterland' included a symbolic drawing *(opposite page)*. Dr. von Gudden had been buried two days previously, no member of the royal family had been present. This was forbidden by etiquette since the King had not yet been buried. The 'Neueste Nachrichten' wrote: "For hours afterwards people grouped together silently at the tomb of the famous doctor and savant who left this life as a selfless servant, loyal to the King and to his noble profession".

cession to the throne requires legitimate progeny issuing from marriage of equal rank authorized by the King". Max Sydel (Bavarian State Legislation) states: "The succession requirements set down in the Constitution are exhaustive. Unfitness to rule is not a hindrance to succession". On the day after Ludwig's burial Anton Memminger, publisher of the 'Unabhängige Bayerische Landeszeitung', an independent newspaper, wrote: "To maintain its position and to continue its ineffectual rule, the Lutz Ministry has declared Prince Otto as King. The Constitution requires that the King must swear an oath of allegiance to the Constitution. Should the Prince, who is not capable of swearing an oath as he can neither read nor uphold this oath, now be fit to be King? The Ministry has appointed the Regent for its own ends". Memminger was prosecuted and sentenced to two months imprisonment for 'insulting' the Ministry. In a dark damp cell in the old prison at Würzburg he became ill and was later brought to the edge of ruin by confiscation of his property, fines and court costs.

The Funeral

The funeral procession turning into Karlsplatz at the Alter Botanischer Garten *(above)*. In the background the 'glass palace'. Thousands lined the streets. A place at a window cost a hundred gold marks. After the hearse followed the Prince-Regent, Crown Prince Friedrich of Prussia and Rudolf of Austria, princes, archdukes, nobility, state officials and the normal populace. As the coffin was carried into the church, St. Michaels Hofkirche, the clear sky clouded over, there was thunder and lightning and a short shower. The people were struck with awe and the newspapers wrote: "The heavens shed a tear". *Opposite page:* The burial ceremony in St. Michaels Hofkirche, in the foreground the entrance to the tomb. Two postscripts: Captain Sonntag from Füssen, who had arrested the state commission but then ensured their safe departure from Hohenschwangau, was dishonourably discharged and died of sorrow a year later. Graf Dürckheim, who was openly supported by friends and members of the Court, was acquitted on 14th July 1886 of high treason after an embarrassing trial. Bismarck had immediately interceded on his behalf. Dürckheim was transferred to Metz but his career did not suffer. He died in 1912 as a General-in-Command.

KÖNIGLICHE TAFEL

München, 21. 6. 1886

Ochsenschweifsuppe

Königseeforellen

mit Bearnaiser Tunke

Kalbsrücken

mit gefüllten Champignons

Fleischpastetchen

nach Richelieu

Hühnerbrüstchen

in Mayonnaise mit Trüffel

Königssorbet

Rehbraten mit Pfeffertunke

Salat und Kompott

Spargel mit Hollandaise

Gebackene „Igel"

mit Weichseln

Gefrorenes aus dem Backofen

*

Above: The funeral repast in the Residenz on the day of the King's burial. It was prepared by the Court Chef Theodor Hierneis.

Above left: King Otto.

Left: Prince-Regent Luitpold.

Opposite page: The genius of immortal fame offers a crown of laurels to the King, surprised during his nightly reading.

Die Proklamation lautet:

Ich Ludwig II. König von Bayern

sehe mich veranlaßt an Mein geliebtes bayerisches Volk und an die gesammte deutsche Nation folgenden

Aufruf

zu erlassen.

Der Prinz Luitpold beabsichtigt sich ohne Meinen Willen zum Regenten Meines Landes zu erheben, und mein bisheriges Ministerium hat durch unwahre Angaben über Meinen Gesundheitszustand Mein geliebtes Volk getäuscht und bereitet hochverrätherische Handlungen vor.

Ich fühle Mich körperlich und geistig so gesund, wie jeder andere Monarch, und der geplante Hochverrath ist so überraschend, daß Mir keine Zeit bleiben wird, Gegenmaßregeln zur Vereitelung der vom Ministerium beabsichtigten Verbrechen zu treffen.

Falls die geplanten Gewaltakte zur Ausführung kommen und Prinz Luitpold ohne Meinen Willen die Regierungsgewalt an sich reißt, beauftrage ich Meine treuen Freunde, mit allen Mitteln und unter allen Umständen meine Rechte zu wahren.

Ich erwarte von allen treuen bayerischen Beamten, insbesondere aber von jedem ehrliebenden bayerischen Offizier und jedem braven bayerischen Soldaten, daß sie eingedenk des heiligen Eides, durch welchen sie Mir Treue gelobt haben, Mir auch in diesen schweren Stunden treu bleiben und Mir im Kampfe gegen die nächststehenden Verräther beistehen werden.

Jeder königstreue Bayer wird aufgefordert, den Prinzen Luitpold und das bisherige Gesammtministerium als Hochverräther zu bekämpfen.

Ich fühle mich mit Meinem geliebten Volk eins und bin der festen Ueberzeugung, daß Mein Volk Mich auch gegen den geplanten Hochverrath schützen wird.

Ich wende mich auch an die gesammte deutsche Nation und an die verbündeten Fürsten.

Soviel in Meiner Macht lag, habe Ich zum Aufbau des deutschen Reiches beigetragen und darf deshalb von der deutschen Nation erwarten, daß sie es nicht duldet, wenn ein deutscher Fürst durch Hochverrath verdrängt wird.

Falls Mir keine Zeit bleiben sollte, Mich an Seine Majestät den deutschen Kaiser direkt um Hilfe zu wenden, dann vertraue Ich der Gerechtigkeit, welche Mir zum Mindesten keinen Widerstand entgegensetzt, wenn Ich die Hochverräther in Meinem Lande den Gerichten überliefere.

Meine braven und treuen Bayern werden Mich sicherlich nicht verlassen, und für den Fall, daß man Mich mit Gewalt verhindern sollte, mein Recht selbst zu wahren, soll dieser Aufruf an jeden treuen Bayer eine Aufforderung sein, sich um Meine treuen Anhänger zu schaaren und an der Bereitelung des geplanten Verraths an König und Vaterland mitzuhelfen.

Gegeben zu Hohenschwangau am 9. Juni 1886.

Ludwig II.,
König von Bayern, Pfalzgraf b. Rh. 2c."

On the King's Death

In the tragic night of Ludwig's death, the marks of coach wheels were discovered in the park. In 1932 a 'royal chamberlain Freiherr von T' brought forward a 'revelation' in which he maintained that two courageous men had, with Empress Elisabeth's knowledge, attempted to help the King escape. The coach had also contained thousands of handbills of the proclamation which Ludwig had composed on 9th June 1886 and in which he accused Prince Luitpold of high treason, calling on all loyal Bavarians "to frustrate the treason planned against the King and country". The gripping wording of the proclamation suggested that Graf Dürckheim had helped formulate it. It appeared at that time in the 'Bamberger Journal' and was distributed as a handbill. The rare copy shown here *(left)* bears the following note *(above)*: "I received the proclamation overleaf on the Museum bridge in Nuremberg on 10th June 1886. Copies were distributed to passers-by by a man whom I did not know. He had apparently distributed but a few handbills when a policeman arrived, prohibited distribution and confiscated the remaining copies. Signed Warnberg".

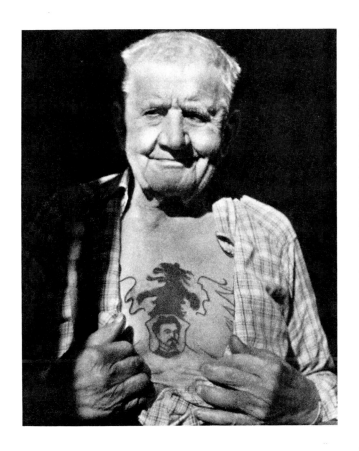

A tattoo of the King on his chest and loyalty in his heart *(above)*. Fritz Schwegler was formerly Ludwig's outrider but he was also unable to illuminate the mystery surrounding Ludwig's death. He saw the body, still clothed, shortly after it had been retrieved from the lake. He noted: "He had not been shot. There was no injury, just water...". Pamphlet followed pamphlet, each claiming to speak the 'truth about the death of the unforgettable Ludwig II. King of Bavaria' *(above right)*. Even though large sections of the populace still believed that Ludwig was alive, fantasy was stimulated by the painting showing the King, with sceptre and crown, at the bottom of Lake Starnberg *(right)*. It was produced in 1887 as a print, together with the following poem. Both were a great success.

EINE VISION

Allnächtlich auf des Sees Grund,
Wenn Luna glänzt in stiller Stund,
Erschauet man ein Königs-Bild,
Fast schemenhaft, im Schilfgefild.

Und händeringend klagt im See
Die schöne Nixe laut ihr Weh. –
Erst wenn der frühe Morgen graut,
Verstummet auch ihr Klagelaut.

Our story would not be complete without this document which only came to light in 1961. It is the second page of a two page document said to have been written by Jakob Lidl, fisher to the King. A translation of the whole document is reproduced on the following page.

A Strange Document

The document is a double sheet of paper, 33 by 21 centimetres, written in pencil. It is said to have been written by Jakob Lidl, fisher to Ludwig II. It was found by chance in 1961 in his estate. In that final tragic night Lidl was wakened by Dr. Müller and was present when Müller and Huber, the castle administrator, found the bodies in the lake. His 'memoirs' begin in the year 1884 but by 1886 he had made only one entry indicating that he was to be conscripted to the pioneers. His conscription was postponed, certainly after consultation with higher powers. In 1885 when the King was seeking funds abroad, he awaited on Ludwig's behalf a visit by 'gentlemen from France'. However, Lutz ordered him to report to the gentlemen that Ludwig was not in residence, "otherwise" continues his entry, "I would be conscripted immediately". In 1886, Dr. von Schleiss, the King's physician, confided to Lidl four days before the King's death: "Imagine, Jakob, they want to declare our King insane, the pack. He is in fine health". It should be noted that Dr. von Schleiss often reiterated this opinion. But now to Lidl's disjointed notes concerning the tragic night of 13th June 1886.

"13th June. I was wakened at 9.30. I thought first of having to help the King to flee. The King's watch, six minutes to seven, Gudden's stopped at 8.10. The King's watch had already disappeared into a gentleman's pocket. The drama is for me like the footprints. At five in the morning investigated footprints with Dr. Heiss from Starnberg, prints one and a half metres apart. No struggle, either King was chloroformed by others or had heart attack. To say King murdered Gudden is totally untrue. Washington was the one who falsified all the telegrams. I was told later that a fisher from Possenhofen, now fisher to the Court in Ammerland, had to put footprints of King and Gudden closer together in the clay bed of the lake. He used a pole with a wooden shoe attached. King was against the Prussians. We fishermen were not allowed to have German flag (black, red and white). We were given the Bavarian flag (white and blue in a diamond pattern). Today mountain folk visited, said I had taken two wax figures from the lake. Telegraphist Mathaus told me they want to rid themselves of the King. He will be declared mad. (The next line is illegible)".

These notes were not written directly after the royal tragedy but perhaps several years later. There are astounding contradictions between this and Eulenburg's version as regards the footprints in the lake. There are also other remarkable differences in the details of the events – quite apart from bold accusations that Washington had "falsified" the telegrams and more. Jakob Lidl, who died in 1933, never spoke a word of the events of that final night. He explained his silence with the ominous suggestion: "It would have been easy to put me away into an asylum".

If his version is true, then exciting new perspectives would be opened up. But whatever documents, ingenuity and fantasy may attempt to prove, the last hours of Ludwig II remain a dark mystery.

"Speak not of this", a painting by A. de Courten, 1887. It warned to leave the dead King with his secret.

König Ludwig II. nimmt am
Morgen des 11. Juni 1886 aus den Händen der Frau Posthalter Vogl in Seeshaupt das letzte Glas Wasser entgegen.

The Proof of Love

Man halte die Karte zirka 50 cm vom Gesicht entfernt, betrachte genau den weissen Punkt an der Nase und zähle dabei bis 30. Dann sehe man sogleich an eine weisse Wand oder Decke, wo nach kurzer Zeit König Ludwig II. erscheint.

Much had been said of the wasteful extravagance of the King and of the fact that he turned his back on the world. Now, all was forgotten, again he was the brilliant monarch of old. Prince-Regent Luitpold, who had been badly advised to support Ludwig's deposition instead of leaving such affairs to the Ministry (which, in any case, was afraid of turning public opinion against itself even more), had long to wait before gaining the confidence of the people. However, it was just good-natured teasing to call him 'potato face' on account of his bucolic, wrinkled features. How different had Ludwig been. Glorified by his dark fate, he was now known as the legendary King. The first outward sign of the birth of the legend was the popularity of postcards showing Ludwig. The most popular are shown on these two pages.

Left: Hold the card about two feet in front of you. Look at the white spot on the nose and count to 30. Then look immediately at a white wall or ceiling. After a short time King Ludwig will appear.
Opposite page: Contemporary picture postcards commemorating King Ludwig II.

Du brauchst kein
Standbild von Stein,
Du brauchst kein Denkmal aus Erz.
Dein Bild wird ewig leben,
Im treuen Bayernherz.

Verlag v. J. Silberstein, München.

7362

Schloss Herrenchiemsee.

N° 19482 GEBRÜDER METZ TÜBINGEN.

Schloß Berg am Starnberger See.   Votivkapelle.

Bayern trauert

Votiv-Kapelle im Schlosspark zu Berg.   Starnberg mit Blick auf das Gebirge.   GRÜSSE vom STARNBERGER SEE.

Schloss Berg.

Otmar Zieher, München.

The Ludwig Song

A new Ludwig song is included in the repertoire of the 'Waakirchner' group of singers from Tölz. It is performed by them with inimitable grace. A verse of the original German is printed below:

Ach, unser Ludwig, Bayerns Zierde,
er war ein König Zoll für Zoll.
Begabt von edler Herrscherwürde,
sein Lob aus jedem Mund erscholl.
Doch eines bleibt uns unvergeßlich,
drum sei es hier im Lied erwähnt:
die stolzen himmelblauen Augen,
die jeder Wittelsbacher kennt!

'Barbarn' in verse 3 means barbarians. 'Bandarsch' in verse 4 are bonds and the expression. 'Kloroformen' as used in verse 4 means to anaethetize with chloroform. There are two similar, original versions of this song. This third version is still sung today in Bavaria with heartfelt sincerity.

Two recast verses of the "Ludwig Song" give Bimarck the blame for Ludwig's death. This popular version runs as follows:

Dr. Gudden und der Bismarck/den man auch den falschen Kanzler nennt/haben's ihn in See hineingestessen/indem sie ihn von hinten angerennt!/Feiger Kanzler, deine Schande/ bringet dir ganz gwiss kein Ehrenpreis/denn du kämpfest nicht im offenen Kampfe/wie der Rippenstoss von hinten her beweist!

This version is still current. It has been passed down as an example of the way in which the legend of Ludwig II has been and is still being kept alive. There are still many pictures and much bric-à-brac which bear witness to his popularity. Examples are shown *(above)*: the King's portrait on the lid of a beer stein and "King Ludwig Coffee". It is no surprise that the life and death of the legendary King are the subject of many a film. In 1930 Ludwig was played by Wilhelm Dieterle. In 1965 an "unforgettable" performance was provided by O. W. Fischer as Ludwig with Ruth Leuwerik as Empress Elisabeth *(left)*. Since then further Ludwig films have been produced – some with fanciful tricks which have not been to the liking of Ludwig followers. Of the more recent literature on the subject of Ludwig II, the novelle "Vergittertes Fenster" by Klaus Mann (S. Fischer Verlag, 1960) is worthy of mention; in this version the royal drama is depicted as a mythical ballad.

Ludwig II – shot whilst trying to escape?

What really happened on the shore and in the waters of Lake Starnberg on that rain-drenched, storm-whipped night of Whit Sunday, 13th June 1886, still occupies the minds of many. The King and Dr. Gudden were alone when they met their deaths – and their deaths gave rise to the most fantastic rumours. Many such rumours have succeeded only in shrouding in further mystery the dramatic events of that night – or in illuminating only the aspects of a medieval assassination. Some versions are worthy of closer investigation but firstly we shall hear the testimony of a man who was present when the bodies were found.

Previously unpublished report of an eye witness

In the "Handschriften-Sammlung der Stadtbibliothek Monacensia" there is a 'true report of the King Ludwig catastrophe' by Jakob Wimmer, the castle administrator at Berg. For a better understanding of the following extracts it is necessary to identify the persons mentioned. Dr. Müller was Gudden's assistant, Huber was a second castle administrator, Schuster and Liebmann were servants and Gumbiller was a kitchen help. The fisher Lidl and Jakob Wimmer himself were the other members of a group of seven who came closest to witnessing the final tragedy. Wimmer writes that the dead King "lay in the water, both hands almost touching the lake bed, his back projected out of the water. Lidl said that the lake was no more than a yard deep at that point, whereupon Huber and Gumbiller jumped into the lake, lifted Ludwig's body and cried, "The King, the King". Lidl drove both oars into the lake bed to anchor the boat. Huber and Gumbiller lifted the body whilst Dr. Müller and Liebmann pulled it into the boat".

Dr. Müller made immediate attempts at resuscitation but to no avail. Huber despatched Wimmer and Schuster to the castle to fetch a stretcher, and Huber it was who thrust a branch into the bed of the lake to mark the spot where they had found the King. The boat was turned and almost collided with the body of Dr. von Gudden, floating in the water nearer to the shore but in the same bent fashion as Ludwig's body. It was carried to the shore by Huber and Gumbiller, and thence to a ground-floor room in the castle. Meanwhile the boat bearing the King's body had reached the shore. The body was placed on an improvised stretcher with a mattress, blanket and pillow and carried by six men to the blue bedroom on the second floor. Wimmer reported: "Again Dr. Müller attempted resuscitation, and also made cuts on the soles of his feet, but again in vain. We then prepared the bed as a bed of state and brought candles from the chapel, about twelve in all."

The next morning the total populace of the region gathered before the castle... "threatening to enter by force" and saying, "if the King is dead, then not one of us will leave the house alive". Eventually the people were calmed and the wait for Empress Elisabeth continued. She was the first to

Ludwig II struggling with Dr. von Gudden in the shallow waters of Lake Starnberg

kneel before Ludwig's dead body. She placed a jasmine bouquet upon his breast and, tearfully, kissed his forehead. Hardly had she departed than all present forced their way into the room causing the servants to flee to safety. "The people did not wish to leave the room. Most took souvenirs, many cut pieces from the furniture. The linen cloth on which the King lay was torn to shreds for souvenirs. Had Gudden not died with the King and had he returned without the King, he would have been beaten to death by the excited crowd. His body had to be protected but was nevertheless jabbed and spit upon."

This is an eye witness report by Jakob Wimmer. He, and the other servants, were present at the post-mortem in Munich but his 'true report' does not make the slightest mention of a shot wound or of the blood-drenched clothing of the King.

The castle servants were certainly mentally robust enough to overcome the excitement of the events but later Gumbiller is said to have tried to drown himself in the waters of the Isar. Schuster is reported to have been committed to a mental institution and to have died shortly afterwards. The Wimmer report does not mention the servant Hartinger who is said to have suffered the same fate. Nor had Wimmer noticed the presence of at least two armed policemen in the park that last night. One died a mysterious death, the other, furnished with a large sum of money, disappeared for ever to America. The statements of these policemen were no less mysterious. They both saw and heard "Nothing, absolutely nothing". If the King was shot, there must have been traces of blood. On the shore there was a boat-house (this is hardly ever mentioned). It is suggested that the King was shot, hidden there, washed and then placed in the water. This rumour was lent credence by the fact that the boathouse was torn down shortly after the catastrophe. The version that one policeman saw two figures struggling in the water and shot them "accidentally" after having given a warning was never taken seriously. The "blood-soaked waistcoat" of the King still haunts the minds of many – as does the assertion that this and other items of Ludwig's clothing were burnt later in the courtyard of Nymphenburg palace. A Wittelsbacher prince aired this secret to a friend shortly before his death so that he could die in peace. Another rumour has it that a lady-in-waiting surprised the fisher Lidl with the direct question, "The King was shot, wasn't he?". Lidl, taken aback, replied, "Yes, how do you know? I thought I was the only one who knew". In his book "Gewitter am See" the author Wolfgang Christlieb had both the King and Dr. Gudden shot, but he had made full use of poetic licence. He could just as well have had Ludwig kidnapped and taken to the Balkans (this was also rumoured). Christlieb was also reproducing folk legend when he depicted how the King and Dr. von Gudden took an underwater stroll on the bed of Lake Starnberger after they had been murdered.

A totally new explanation of the drama was mooted in 1970. Bishop Dr. Johannes Neuhäusler proclaimed in a sermon at the Munich *Michaelskirche* on the 125th anniversary of the birth of the legendary King that Ludwig had been 'drugged'

The witness: castle administrator Jakob Wimmer.

when he met his death. Martin Beck, the then preacher in Aufkirchen, had told him that he had studied the features of Ludwig during the long hours of the deathwatch and that he was convinced that "this man had not drowned". The preacher had often seen the bodies of drowned men and they looked "different from his". Beck also knew of the existence of a letter from Dr. Gudden to his parents in which he revealed that he "always had a means of subduing the King" who was physically superior to him. It could have been that Gudden did use a drug on Ludwig. This coincides with Lidl's version *(page 161)*. "No struggle – either King was chloroformed by others or had heart attack."

These are just a few of the theories on Ludwig's death. Professor Rall, director of the secret Royal Archives, concludes in his biography 'König Ludwig II' (Verlag Schnell & Steiner, Munich and Zurich, 1977): "The report names no cause of death. None of the proposed theories as to his death is conclusive." The death of the legendary King thus remains a mystery that cannot be unravelled. It belongs to Bavaria's living folklore just as his castles and the love reserved for him by his people.

The Commemorative Chapel on the Shore of Lake Starnberg

One day after the tragedy the spot where it occurred was marked with a pole from which fluttered the white-blue flag of Bavaria. Then a simple cross was erected and on the shore Prince Luitpold had a commemorative column built – a 'watchlight' in the gothic style with a spiral, fluted shaft *(below, forefront of illustration)*. Ten years later on 13th June 1896, the Regent presided over the laying of the foundation stone of a 'commemorative chapel' and four years later to the day, the chapel was consecrated. The chapel is in the early romanesque style with a dome-shaped roof and is reminiscent of Ludwig's obsession with the 'grail'. It was designed by the architect Julius Hofmann, who was responsible for completing Neuschwanstein after 1884. In financing the building "the trustees of the assets of King Otto showed a great willingness to accede to the wishes of the Regent". Every year, on the anniversary of Ludwig's death, the 'Verein zur Wiedererrichtung eines Denkmals für König Ludwig II. von Bayern' decorates the cross on the lake *(left)* with a wreath. All year through visitors make the journey to the chapel and many place flowers there.

»Die Woge wallt und prallt zurück,
Ohn' Unterlaß in gleichem Ton:
So wechselt stets das Menschenglück
In Hütte und auf Königsthron.

Doch oben fest die Kirche steht,
Nicht rührt an sie des Lebens Streit,
Erzählt von Treu', die nie vergeht,
Von Gott und seiner Ewigkeit.«

Opposite page: Model of the projected Falkenstein castle, 1884. This was to be the King's "robber knights' castle". Max Schultze, architect to the Prince Thurn und Taxis, drew up the plans. The castle was to stand on the Falkenstein cliff near Pfronten. A road and a water line were led to the cliff top – but no money was available to build the castle itself.

Neuschwanstein towers majestically on its cliff-top, a world-wonder in stone. Built in one of the most beautiful regions of the Bavarian Alps, the castle is a testimony to the noble, romantic nature of the King who sought the grail.

Ludwig II. as a Knight of the Order of St. George, the legendary King as he ruled Bavaria. "In the brilliance of youth, enflamed with idealism, strong and healthy, of a dignity inborn and a serenity of mind . . ." This was the man who won the hearts of his people.

His Fate will not be forgotten:

he was a King and it was his downfall!

In the *Gnadenkirche* at Altötting stands the silver urn *(right)* containing the heart of Ludwig II. Sixty centimetres high, on a base of black marble, the urn bears a bouquet of Alpine roses and edelweiss on each side. The face of the urn is adorned with a crown above the initials LL. The seal on the reverse bears the coat of arms of Bavaria.

Opposite page: Flag bearers of the 'König Ludwig II Trachtenverein' lower their white-blue banners in a symbolic gesture expressing the love and loyalty which Bavarians still afford today to their legendary King of the House of Wittelsbach.

Appendix

Chronology

1845 25 August: Prince Ludwig born to the Bavarian Crown Prince Maximilian and his wife, Marie, a Princess of Prussia.
26 August: christened Otto Ludwig Friedrich Wilhelm on the birthday and name day of his grandfather, Ludwig I (1825–1868).

1848 20 March: Ludwig I abdicates, due to his romance with Lola Montez, in favour of his son Maximilian.
27 April: Ludwig's brother Otto born.
Monarchy limited by a State Basic Law.

1861 16-year-old Ludwig permitted to see his first Wagner opera, 'Lohengrin'.

1864 10 March: death of King Maximilian after short illness. Ludwig II becomes King and takes the traditional oath.
4 May: first meeting with Richard Wagner. Plans for a monumental theatre in Munich.
June: meeting with Elisabeth, Empress of Austria in Bad Kissingen and with the Tsarina of Russia in Bad Schwalbach.

1865 11 May: final rehearsal for Wagner's 'Tristan and Isolde';
10 June: première in the Royal Court and National Theatre in Munich.
10 December: Richard Wagner is forced to leave Munich on the initiation of the Cabinet Secretary Pfistermeister.

1866 Bismarck seeks to drive Austria from the German Confederation. Bavaria makes an unsuccessful attempt to arbitrate between Austria and Prussia.

10 May: after long hesitation, Ludwig signs the order for mobilization and considers abdication for the first time.
22 May: the King, due to open the *Landtag*, departs for a secret visit to Wagner in Switzerland. He holds his Speech from the Throne on 27 May.
3 July: the battle at Königgrätz (Sadowa) is catastrophic for the Austrian army; the Southern Germans clash with the Prussians: civil war.
22 August: peace treaty and aggreement for mutual support with Prussia, without the guarantees demanded by Ludwig II.
10 November: Ludwig II tours the Bavarian provinces ravaged by the war.

1867 22 January: engagement to Sophie, daughter of Herzog Maximilian of Bayern, sister of Empress Elisabeth of Austria.
June: Ludwig II visits the World Exhibition in Paris.
Repeated postponement of the wedding day: 25 August to 12 October, then to 12 November.
10 October: Ludwig II breaks off his engagement.

1868 29 February: death of Ludwig I.
21 June: première of 'The Mastersingers', triumph for Richard Wagner.
August: another meeting with the Tsar and Tsarina of Russia in Bad Kissingen and at Schloss Berg.
First plans for Linderhof and Neuschwanstein.

1869 5 September: foundation stone for Neuschwanstein is laid.
22 September: première of 'Rheingold', part of the 'Ring of the Nibelung'.

1870　15 July: France declares war on Prussia due to Bismarck's 'Ems telegram' of 13 July.
16 July: Ludwig II orders mobilization; joins Prussia in war with France.
Crown Prince Friedrich of Prussia commander of South German troops.
2 September: victory of German army at Sedan, aided by 1st Bavarian Corps, commanded by Freiherr von der Tann. Negotiations with Bismarck on joint constitution.
3 December: 'Kaiserbrief', Ludwig II invites the Prussian King to become Emperor.

1871　18 January: proclamation of the German Emperor in the *Galerie des Glaces* at Versailles.
Bavarian Parliament approves the Versailles agreement.
16 July: victory celebrations in Munich.

1872　22 May: foundation stone of *Festspielhaus* in Bayreuth laid.
Royal hunting lodge built at Schachen.

1873　Ludwig II buys the island Herrenwörth on Chiemsee.

1874　6 May: first of many *Separatvorstellungen* in the *Hoftheater*.
20 August: Ludwig II travels to Versailles as 'Graf von Berg'.
25 August: Emperor Wilhelm I guarantees Bavaria's independence.
Work on the winter garden in the Munich *Residenz*.

1875　Prince Otto's mental condition worsens. He lives in isolation at Fürstenried.

1876　August: Ludwig II present at rehearsals for the 'Ring of the Nibelung' in Bayreuth. Opening of the *Festspielhaus*.
Linderhof completed.

1878　21 May: foundation stone of Herrenchiemsee laid.

1880　700th anniversary of Wittelsbach rule.

1883　13 February: Richard Wagner dies in Venice.

1886　The financial situation worsens; the King cannot raise money for building. The Cabinet funds have to be restored to financial soundness.
8 June: a medical report produced by Dr. von Gudden and two other doctors declares Ludwig II to be "incurably insane and incapable of ruling for the rest of his life".
9 June: Ludwig II is legally incapacitated. The State Commission sent to collect him in Neuschwanstein is arrested.
Graf Dürckheim, the loyal aide-de-camp, is arrested in Munich when trying to protect the King's interests.
Ludwig II refuses to flee and considers suicide.
10 June: Prince Luitpold, the second son of Ludwig I, is declared Regent in place of the incapacitated Ludwig.
11/12 June: Ludwig II is brought at night from Neuschwanstein to Schloss Berg by Dr. von Gudden, another doctor and five warders.
13 June: Ludwig II and Dr. von Gudden do not return from a walk. Both are found dead in Lake Starnberg on the same day.
15 June: Ludwig II is laid in state in the *Hofkapelle*. Thousands pay their last respects.
18 June: the population mourns at Ludwig's funeral.

Sources

There is a wealth of literature on Ludwig II. Only those books are listed here which served as sources for this work.

Jacques Bainville: »Louis II de Bavière«, A. Fayard et Cie., Paris. – Ludwig Below: »Dem Toten die Ehre«, Bayerischer Volksverlag, München. – Gottfried von Böhm: »Ludwig II. von Bayern«, Verlag Hans Robert Engelmann, Berlin, 1922. – Egon Caesar Conte Corti: »Ludwig I. von Bayern«, Bruckmann, München, 1960 (7. Aufl. 1979). – M. Doeberl: »Entwicklungsgeschichte Bayerns«, dritter Band, herausgegeben von Max Spindler, Verlag von R. Oldenbourg, München, 1931. – Corbinian Ettmayr: »Die Gedächtniskapelle für König Ludwig II.«, Verlag der Gesellschaft für christliche Kunst, München, 1901. – Philipp Fürst zu Eulenburg-Hertefeld: »Das Ende König Ludwigs II. und andere Erlebnisse«, Fr. Wilh. Grunow Verlag, Leipzig. – Otto Gerold: »Die letzten Tage von König Ludwig II., Erinnerungen eines Augenzeugen«, Caesar Schmidt Verlag, Zürich, 1903. – Hans Goldschmidt, Hans Kaiser, Hans Thimme: »Ein Jahrhundert Deutscher Geschichte«, Reichsgedanke und Reich, 1815–1919. Verlag von Reimar Hobbing, Berlin, 1928. – Maximilian Harden: »Köpfe«, Erich Reiß Verlag, Berlin, 1911. – Louise von Kobell: »König Ludwig II. von Bayern und die Kunst«, Kunstverlag von Jos. Albert, München, 1898. – Heinrich Kreisel: »Die Schlösser Ludwigs II. von Bayern«, Franz Schneekluth Verlag, Darmstadt. – Friedrich Rudolph Kreuzer: »Unser Bayernland in Wort und Bild«, Commissionsverlag von Ernst Wiest Nachf., Leipzig. – Fritz Linde: »Ich, der König«, Der Untergang Ludwigs des Zweiten. Georg Kummer's Verlag, Leipzig, 1926. – Klaus Mann: »Vergittertes Fenster«, Novelle um den Tod des Königs Ludwig II. von Bayern. S. Fischer Verlag, 1960. – Anton Memminger: »Der Bayernkönig Ludwig II.«, Gebrüder Memminger, Würzburg, 1919. – Franz Carl Müller: »Die letzten Tage König Ludwigs II. von Bayern«, nach eigenen Erlebnissen geschildert, Fischer's Medicin, Berlin, 1888. – Eugen Müller-Münster: »Elisabeth Ney«, Verlag Koehler und Amelang, Leipzig, 1931. – Guy de Pourtalès: »König Hamlet«, Ludwig II. von Bayern. Urban-Verlag, Freiburg i. Br., 1929. – Hans Reidelbach: »Luitpold, Prinzregent von Bayern«, Reidelbach'scher Verlag, München, 1892. – Werner Richter: »Ludwig II. König von Bayern«, Bruckmann, München, 1958 (10. Aufl. 1982). – Walter Rummel: »König und Kabinettchef.« Aus den Tagen Ludwigs II., Franz Hanfstaengl, München, 1919. – Walter Schmidkunz: »Das leibhaftige Liederbuch«, Gebr. Richters Verlagsanstalt, Erfurt, 1938. – Hans Thoma: »Amtliche Führer« der Bayerischen Verwaltung der Staatlichen Schlösser, Gärten und Seen, München. – Karl Tschuppik: »Elisabeth, Kaiserin von Österreich«, Verlag Dr. Hans Epstein, Wien und Leipzig, 1929. – Karl Winterfeld: »Vollständige Geschichte des Deutsch-Französischen Krieges von 1870/71«, Gustav Hempel, Berlin, 1871. – Paul Wiegler: »Josef Kainz«, Deutscher Verlag, Berlin, 1941. – Georg Jakob Wolf: »König Ludwig II. und seine Welt«, Franz Hanfstaengl, München, 1926.

Illustrations

The numbers refer to the sum of works.
National and municipal museums and collections:
Bayerische Verwaltung der Staatlichen Schlösser, Gärten und Seen, München, 29 und Farbbilder Seite 17, 68, 69, 89, 97. – Bundesbahndirektion Nürnberg, Eisenbahnmuseum, 2. – Staatliche Münzsammlung, München, 2. – Stadtmuseum München, 39. – Theatermuseum, Clara-Ziegler-Stiftung, München, 16.
Photographers, photo archives, private collections and publishers:
Lala Aufsberg, Sonthofen im Allgäu, 12. – Gloria-Film, 1. – Harro Dau, München, 4. – Li Erben, München, 13. – Historisches Bildarchiv Handke-Berneck, 9. – Franz Hanfstaengl, München, 18. – J. Heigenhauser, 1. – M. Herpich, München, Farbbild Seite 131. – Theodor Hierneis: »Der König speist«, im Heimeran-Verlag, München, 1. – H. Huber, Garmisch-Partenkirchen, Farbbild Seite 115. – Dr. A. Jüthner, Siegsdorf, 13. – Keystone, Int. Presseagentur, München, 2. – Löbl-Schreyer, Bad Tölz, Farbbild Seite 96. – Werner Neumeister, München, Farbbilder Seite 100/101, 130. – Sammlung N. H. 1. – »Münchener Punsch«, 3. – Wolfgang Schade: »Europäische Dokumente«, Union Deutsche Verlagsgesellschaft, Stuttgart, 2. – T. Schneiders, Lindau, Farbbild Seite 115. – Rupert Stöckl, München, 13 und Farbbilder Seite 35, 61, 163. – Albert Widemann, Mühltal, 2. – All other pictures and documents were supplied by Bruckmann Verlag or the author.

The author would like to extend his special thanks to all the museums, collections and administrative offices mentioned above for their kind help, as well as to the publishers Franz Hanfstaengl and Dr. A. Jüthner, Rupert Stöckl, Fritz Schwegler and Albert Widemann.